Divine Purpose

WITH GOD, NO TRIAL
IS EVER WASTED

Donya Gonzalez

TRILOGY CHRISTIAN PUBLISHERS

TUSTIN, CA

Trilogy Christian Publishers
A Wholly Owned Subsidary of Trinity Broadcasting Network
2442 Michelle Drive
Tustin, CA 92780

Divine Purpose

Trilogy Christian Publishers
A Wholly Owned Subsidiary of Trinity Broadcasting Network
2442 Michelle Drive Tustin, CA 92780

Manufactured in the United States of America

10 9 8 7 6 5 4 3 2 1

Library of Congress Cataloging-in-Publication Data is available.

ISBN: 978-1-68556-905-1

E-ISBN: 978-1-68556-906-8

Dedication

To my family (that includes you too, J. J.): thank you for your support and love throughout this process. To my husband: thank you for your incredible courage in allowing me to share such personal parts of our lives.

Shout out to my daughter, Gabby: you, my dear, are a rock star and one tough cookie! Thank you for not letting me slack off.

To my dad: my biggest regret is that we never got to collaborate on a book project, but I know you are proud of your baby girl. You had a great deal to do with my passion for reading and writing. Love you, Daddy!

Introduction

My prayer is that this book speaks to your spirit and sets you free.

I share my story because secrets are the poison that eats away at your soul.

God has a divine purpose for the things that He does, even if we don't think it's divine. Resting in the palm of God's hand is like going through a category-six hurricane or a major fire, and none of the battering winds or destructive flames can touch you. "He will keep him in perfect peace whose mind is stayed on Him" (Isaiah 26:3, paraphrased).

Scripture says in Psalm 18:30, "As for God, His way is perfect; The word of the LORD is proven; He is a shield to all who trust in Him." It doesn't mean that we will have an easy time, but that everything God allows us to go through is to either strengthen our faith or draw us closer to Him, and while we experience the ups and downs of life, God is right there, shielding us from the enemy. How could we not trust Him?

This past year has been like standing in a room that's been set on fire and watching it burn down all around me. Can you imagine it? The scorching heat, the smoke that chokes the oxygen from your lungs and burns your eyes so that only tears flow from them, blurring your vision. The flames are so hot that it feels as if your skin is melting, and your hair feels as if every strand is made of fire. The flames devouring everything in their path are so powerful that nothing stands a chance against them, and there you stand in the midst, watching it all burn down around you, powerless to stop it. Watching the flames eat away at everything—the walls, roof—all falling to the ground like rain, you could feel the heat, smell the smoke, and yet your eyes don't burn, and your clothes are not singed. That is because we serve an awesome God who will not leave or forsake us, and just like with the three Hebrew boys, He is in the midst, with us.

I felt as if I was flame-retardant from head to toe, and though I could see what was going on, the damaging flames didn't affect me. I felt as if I was made of Teflon because the blood of Jesus covers and protects me and the Great I Am speaks over me!

You stand on the only real estate in the room untouched by the flame, panicking to find a way out, but every entryway and exit is blocked by the scorching flames, and you see no way out—that is, until you look up.

When you put yourself in the palm of the hand of the One who controls it all, "no evil shall befall you, nor shall any plague come near your dwelling" (Psalm 91:10). God is faithful to His word. When you are His, you are under divine protection; that's the prime real estate we stand on when we are Christians: we stand on Christ, the solid rock.

August 15, 2021

The Winepress

Sometimes God will allow us to experience troubles and trials that may seem to bring us to the brink of breaking, but there is a purpose to everything God does. He will allow a situation to happen to expose things that He wants to change in us or resolve in our lives. I began to understand this fact as things started to happen in mine. The process is difficult, sometimes even painful, and it stinks, but we must go through it to get to the healing that God has for each of us.

We had a drain field that was not functioning properly and was causing a plumbing problem inside the house. You could not wash a load of laundry or take a shower without the dreaded gurgling in every drain of the house—a warning of the disaster to come, followed by a noxious fume that would fill the house. We tried to manage it by timing our daily showers and being strategic about when and how much we did laundry, but eventually, the septic tank was full, and we faced the threat of sewage backing up into the house. So, we called a company to come to pump out our septic tank.

When the company came, they emptied the tank in a matter of minutes; however, when we were asked to flush the toilets in the house to make sure everything was functioning again, one of our toilets would not flush. We tried several times, but the plumber had to come inside and use a plunger to clear the toilet drain manually while his partner used a giant vacuum to clear the drain from within the septic tank. The guy had to use so much force while he plunged the toiled that he had to use two hands and leverage his foot on the bathtub because the clog would not budge. The worker outside had to push the vacuum hose into the drainpipe at the same time to clear it. Finally, with both working together, they got the drain cleared, and everything was flowing again.

I tell this story because this is what happens when we bottle up feelings or ignore matters in our lives that God wants us to face. It could be a marriage on the rocks where one person ignores the fact that they have not been the spouse the other deserves, an injured party holding on to slights and mistreating the other, or something that, if left unchecked, has the potential to destroy. Eventually, these things create problems in our lives, whether it be health issues, marital or relationship ones, and we are forced to deal with the smelly mess.

Like in the situation with the clog, ignoring it only causes the problem to fill every area of your life until it is, eventually, spilling out and ruining everything it touches. It takes us to work in tandem with God to clear out the mess and allow His healing to flow through us. God desires the best for His children, and sometimes His "best" means working on the things that we want to keep buried away or ignore. He does not want the enemy to have any weapons to use against us. Think about it: if you do not face that thing that happened in your past that causes you to feel insecure, every time you find yourself in a situation that triggers that insecurity, it will tear you down and take you down a path that draws you away from God.

It was a Tuesday night, almost midnight, and I could not sleep, so I put on YouTube, looking for a sermon to inspire and feed me before I drifted off to sleep. Everything I saw was ten or fifteen minutes long, but I wanted something beefier, something more. A video popped up with Bishop T. D. Jakes during his appearance on TBN about his book *Crushing*. I had purchased the study guide for *Crushing* weeks before, thinking I had the book but had confused it with one of the bishop's other books, and my daughter laughed at me, saying I bought the study guide and did not know that I did not have the book, but this was divine.

I watched the first twenty minutes, but it became too much, so I turned it off, intending to finish it later, not realizing that a day or two later, I would be placed in the winepress, and my world and how I saw it would change forever. I couldn't understand why it was so difficult for me to watch, but in hindsight, I realize the Holy Spirit was leading me to this message because He knew the impending storm that was on the horizon, and in my spirit, I didn't want to face whatever was coming.

My husband woke up the next morning and was looking at me in such a way that I knew he was holding onto something. A few weeks before, he had looked at me the same way, and when I questioned him, he said he was fine. This morning he looked at me like someone holding onto nausea roiling in their stomach so that they would not vomit.

I said to him, "What? What is it?" and then he dropped a bomb on me that would reverberate into my past and try to shatter my future. He cheated. I knew it all along in my spirit, but he had always denied it when I would ask him if he was ever unfaithful—lied for the better part of twenty years. He had not just cheated once but three times: once before we were married and twice after the marriage.

However, a strange calm settled over me, as if I was relieved he had finally admitted something I knew all along but could not prove. But that was not it. God had been preparing me for this moment. He had been correcting some of my behaviors, encouraging me, and, most of all, giving me a supernatural peace that He knew I would need to handle such a revelation. The old me would have created a firestorm, which was what my husband expected; instead, what he got was peaceful forgiveness. Now, I did not just forgive him, and everything went back to normal, but rather I forgave him, and the real work began. I had to let the Holy Spirit guide me and allow God to lead me beside His still waters so that I could be restored, so that our marriage could be restored.

God is an amazing multitasker. While He was working on one thing, our marriage, He was working on a few others. He made me go to counseling because I knew that there was a root cause to all of this and that if God was going to deliver me, I needed to be all in and fully committed to my own healing. Being "all in" meant that I had to be brave enough to face the insecurities, careless words spoken by others throughout my life, which created an inferiority complex, and traumas that I held onto that shaped who I was in life and in my relationship. I needed to uproot the lies that I had been told by the enemy and believed ("not good enough," "not smart enough," "not worthy") and needed to allow God to restore my thinking and renew my mind.

I had no idea where to start, but I can tell you, friend: God was laying the foundation years before. Back in 2013, I had a job that required me to travel to Texas to assess and transition the billing team of a company that we had acquired. There I met someone who would change my life forever by leading me to God and the Word. I had traveled to Texas on three different occasions, and the more time I spent with my friend, the more God was laying the foundation for one of the most important relationships in my life! She listened to me and spent hours on the phone, talking me off the ledge when I did some of the craziest things in my marriage out of anger. She told me how much Jesus loved me and has been giving wise counsel to me ever since. God's ways are higher than our ways (Isaiah 55:8–9); we do not always see the big picture, but He always gives us what we need even before we are aware of what it is.

What I would like to share with you are my daily-journal entries that encapsulate much of what I have experienced with spiritual attacks while I was going through this upheaval in my marriage, individual counseling, and navigating living in a home with a person who wrecked a relationship that I thought meant something. I want you to see how God truly gives you beauty for ashes and that the pain you experience when going through trials is never wasted.

August 16, 2021

Psalm 18:30 says, "As for God, His way is perfect; The word of the LORD is proven; He is a shield to all who trust Him." That right there is everything to me! How could I not trust in Him? "For who is God, except the LORD? And who is a rock, except our God?" (Psalm 18:31). Jesus is the solid foundation that we are to build our faith upon—our safe haven.

Psalm 18:39 says, "For You have armed me with strength for the battle; You have subdued under me those who rose up against me." Friend, God has already equipped us for the battles we face, defeated the enemy, and handed him over to us. We have a part to play in that we must take up our weapons (the Word) and fight.

You cannot receive the deliverance that God has for you if you are still holding onto hurt and pain. It's like holding something in one hand and reaching forth with the other for something that we should use both hands to grasp. You cannot hold onto both because you will have to let one go. I realized that I could not hold onto the damage and the brokenness and grasp the healing and wholeness that Jesus had for me. I chose to give it all to God and trust that His plans and purposes for my life are perfect, and in that, there is an amazing peace that came with my letting go and letting God fight my battles for me—that was my role.

God's Word says that He is close to the brokenhearted, but it all still hurts. The beauty is that He knows what hurts us and offers comfort that we cannot find anywhere else but in Him. So, what has the potential to destroy us hurts but for a time.

Of course, the embarrassment came, and I did not want anyone to know, to be known as the woman whose husband cheated on her, and she was stupid enough to stay. This is how the enemy attacks when we are most vulnerable, telling us lies that we are so eager to believe because it feeds our flesh. All of this is a byproduct of pride. It hurts the ego to admit to the world that the perfect façade is just that—a cover-up, a false pretense. Pride is the killer of growth and healing. When we seek to hide things or keep secrets, we stunt our spiritual growth and defer the healing that God has for us.

I took my rings off today. I see them differently, as if they represent a lie. Again, the fool...a reminder that I was in this relationship all by myself, the only one believing in the vows we made.

Every girl dreams of a Prince Charming—we all know the fairy tale about the "happily ever after." The man gets on one knee, confesses his undying love, and asks for your hand. You happily plan a wedding, fully expecting to ride off into the sunset, clutching your "happily ever after." No one tells you to plan for the "what if?"

Just like no one can prepare you for being a parent for the first time (you can take classes, you can read the *What to Expect*

When You're Expecting books), but who prepares you for when life happens? How does one prepare oneself for marriage when two imperfect people come together to create life? Build a life? You cannot be ready for every situation in a marriage that comes in like a wrecking ball when the other person is doing the damage. But with God, all things are possible when we completely trust and give all control over to Him.

When you're the one giving a sort of marriage ultimatum (either marriage or going your separate ways), garnering a pseudo proposal out of fear, when you're the only one taking those vows seriously—who prepares for that?

Today was a rough day. I struggle with this mess that is my marriage. My husband and I had a talk, and I told him that when he confessed to me, I forgave him. I forgave him because, by this time in my walk with Christ, God had done so much work in me that there was no room in my heart for the love I felt, that I was forgiven of my sins and brought into the body of Christ and the unforgiveness that my husband expected when he confessed. He said it meant a lot to him and that he was afraid that I might have hit him or ran off and left him; perhaps, the old vengeful me would have, but all of that was purged from me, and he was relieved, but I was left with the hurt of the betrayal.

I took the opportunity to tell him that over the course of our twenty-year marriage, he had always made me feel as if I didn't matter, didn't have worth, and I had no help from him, as if I couldn't depend on him because he never had my back. When my back was against the wall, I was forced to figure a way out or how to come out swinging because he would just leave me to fend for myself and the children. After we had spoken, he was sitting, eating lunch, and he looked over at me and said, "There were four," and I said, "What?" He held up four fingers and just said, "There were four, not three." I was honestly confused, and then he said, "God told me...He just brought it back from my memory that there was another one," as if he were detached from the thing that he had done that took a wrecking ball to what was left of our marriage, which, from the beginning, was never really a marriage, not in the way God's Word describes marriage as a covenant where a man is to leave his mother and father and cling to his wife, and they are to become one flesh—not many "flesh" with a few affairs sprinkled in between but two parts in one whole.

This new revelation, for some reason, hit me like a punch to the gut. I compared it to someone getting cut open for surgery and, a few weeks later, whilst healing is underway, having the surgeon come back, saying, "Oh wait, I forgot something," and cutting you open again. You start all over again—the pain, the doubt, the broken heart, the healing—everything cut open and raw again. I felt like asking God, "Can I go back and choose not to forgive?"

My husband confessed to cheating and swore it was three persons (one of whom I knew and worked with off and on for ten years, even had her as a friend on Facebook), but I know forgiveness is more for me than for him. The first step to healing is forgiveness and letting go of the thing that hurt you. It did not mean that I did not have questions, just that I would no longer allow this thing that he had done to have its way with my emotions and open me up to spiritual attacks.

Forgiveness allows you to take power back from the enemy and render his tricks and schemes useless. While this is only the beginning of healing, I feel so at peace that whatever my husband did won't break me because my Father has me in the palm of His hands and His Word is absolutely true. I feel that grief, devastation, hurt, anger, and brokenness cannot reach me because God truly has me hidden in His secret place, in His pavilion.

I almost wanted to laugh when my husband told me that he was afraid to tell me he had committed adultery numerous times during our marriage because he did not know if I would yell, hit him, slap him, beat him up, or run out of the house; instead, I was calm. Friend, I must tell you God has truly been preparing me for this for quite some time because even before I was ever walking with God and had a real relationship, God never allowed me to be ignorant. We are the ones who choose to ignore the warning signs.

The very first infidelity came early on in our relationship when we were dating, and he went on a boat cruise with a group of my coworkers whom he got to know through his friend who worked with me and through me. He cheated with a nurse who I worked with from one company to another over decades. Another coworker came back and told me how they were behaving on the boat, and when I confronted him about it, he lied...and continued lying for two decades. Over the years, the memory would come back to me, and my husband kept lying about it. He had cheated on me before we were married and betrayed me after the marriage.

What hit me was not the women but the fact that my husband did not respect the commitment we made before God.

Neither of us did, if I am being honest. Though I was faithful, a few years into our marriage, I lost respect for him because I found myself taking on the responsibility for the children and our family because he could not handle the burden.

I took my rings off today because, for some reason, this fourth admission hit differently. The Holy Spirit told me when my husband said he had been unfaithful with that one person and I said, "I knew it!" that there was more. I asked him again, and he had to admit that it had happened three times. Again, the Holy Spirit said, "There's more," and again, my husband said, "No, there were only three"—this was the day he confessed.

Today he admitted there was a fourth. I asked when these incidences happened, and again, he said when he traveled for work a very long time ago. I asked if it had been the same person because if yes, that would make it a relationship, right? He said no, they were one-night stands in hotels while he traveled. So, he was never really committed, never honored the vows we made, and never cherished our family or me. Then it hit me: he had never worn his wedding ring at the beginning of our marriage and for the better part of fifteen years. I questioned him at the time, and he said that the ring was causing a callous on his hand when he worked and that was why he could not wear it.

So, I asked him today for the truth, "Why did you not wear your ring all those years ago?" And he said it was because he did not want anyone to know he was married. I don't know why, but that statement hit me hard, more than the infidelity, because, to me, all I heard was that he never wanted this marriage; I wasn't important enough to be acknowledged or claimed. I felt like a fool, a fool for keeping a commitment to someone who was not worth it.

Then God spoke to me; He cut through the tears that seemed to come from deep in my soul and said, "You were not honoring your commitment to him; you were honoring your commitment to Me," stopping me in my tracks! What an amazing God we serve that He takes the time to reach out to us when we are hurting to wrap His loving arms around us in comfort.

So, yeah, I took my rings off today because they represented a lie, a sham, a broken covenant, and I swapped them out for a set of rings that I purchased on Amazon because I wanted to honor my commitment to God. I prayed, "Lord, only You can help me through this. I am flying blind in unfamiliar territory and can't navigate these treacherous waters without You. Heal my brokenness, Father, in Jesus's name. Amen!"

August 17, 2021

Trust in God: He and Only He Delivers!

I woke up feeling a bit irritable. I had a difficult time falling asleep, and my husband came to me at about 7:15 a.m., saying that God told him to take another day off because yesterday was good for him and because God had more work to do in him. God has told my husband that he keeps going back to the past, going through the things he asked forgiveness for. I do believe that God spoke to him; God speaks to His children in many ways: we need only listen and pay attention. My husband told me that God said it was okay to take time off because He would provide for us not to worry about not being paid for the time off. I must say I was annoyed, which I knew was the enemy, because why was he getting a word from God after what he had done to me? Why am I the responsible one going to work and making sure I get paid?

God reminded me that it is a choice! He told me to do the same, so tomorrow and on Thursday, I am taking off.

Today brought a bit of anger with it. I was angry that I took care of my husband for ten years while he went through his midlife crisis and did not work. I wore my rings, signifying I was married, while he roamed around as if he was free and single. I took on his garbage as if it were mine and thought I had a problem or was the problem in our marriage, but he was covering up and hiding a lie. I feel like a fool because I wasted twenty-five years with someone not worth my time because, deep down, I had my own insecurities, thinking that he was my only chance at being married. Every relationship I have ever had turned out to be unhealthy, and I believed I was the common denominator. Why can't I get it right? I settled for Ishmael because I didn't wait for Isaac; I did not trust God. Why me?

These are all lies, pressure points, pain points, and triggers that the enemy wants to use against me so that I stay broken, hurt, stuck, and angry. The enemy wants me to keep reopening those same wounds, feeding like a parasite on my pain. Each day, God is exposing things that I need to address in my life: this anger, insecurity, and pain—where does it come from?

It's 2:19 p.m., and my husband is talking to me and joking around like in the old times. As if he did not just turn my world upside down and leave me with a bag full of pain and broken pieces!

A song came on the radio, and the opening line was "I am guilty..." and he changed the station right away.

Look at how God gets in our faces to reveal to us the messy areas of our lives that we need to clean up! We must be honest with ourselves and say, "Yes, I was wrong. What can I do to fix it?"

Trust God and allow Him to show you the way. God's way means recognizing that we have a part to play and have to do whatever we need to in the natural (counseling, talking to a friend or pastor) so that God can move in the spiritual and do the work in us that gets us to a place of healing.

August 19, 2021

That time between sleep and awakeness, around twilight, I thought about where my brokenness really started. And I thought about why and how that could have happened when my dad treated us as if we were each special and favored. I suppose when I was younger, I did not really know what being a favorite child meant.

God brought to my memory, in the midst of it all, that the root word of "favorite" is "favor." The root word "favor" means "gaining approval," "acceptance," or "special benefits or blessings." The Greek word for "favorite" is *eklektos*, meaning "select," "picked out," "chosen," "of those chosen out by God for the rendering of special service to Him." The word is derived from eklegoma, meaning to "select," "choose," "properly selected, especially as a deeply personal choice," literally, "chosen, out of a personal preference (intention)."[1]

God wanted me to know that I was favored and set apart long before my dad favored me. The hurt and damage started early on when I felt I failed at keeping up with a competitive sibling. I felt I was not as smart, athletic, accomplished, or popular, so

I faded into the background, allowing the other person to take center stage because my warped perception of things made me think that I did not measure up. The other person got the attention in the room, and that somehow made me quiet, self-conscious, and reserved. A few adults around us made it clear to me that my sibling was their favorite and obviously treated me differently. That is where the seed was planted and took root, making me feel that there was something about the other person that I did not have.

My mother would tell the story of the time that I gave away all my jewelry at the age of four, and for years, we would all laugh about it. I have a godmother who doted on me as a child and spent money over the years on expensive jewelry for me. I had amassed quite a bit, and my mother kept it in a cute little musical jewelry box. I took the box to school one day without my mother's knowledge and gave away every piece of the jewelry. My mother, when she found out, spanked me and, no doubt, gave me a stern talking-to. She was never able to recover any of the jewelry because none of the parents made their children return it.

All these years, I laughed at the story but never realized the magnitude of it. Why, at four years old, was I so desperate to be accepted and fit in that I felt I could not just make friends but "buy" them? That is the bigger and more concerning part of this scenario. The core of it was the lack of feeling I was enough.

I am amazed that when God is showing us something, we see things more clearly. It is as if we see things with fresh eyes, and He pulls back the covers to reveal what is really going on; He reveals the truth. He brought this to my memory like a mirror in front of my face, showing me what I had missed all these years.

At 9:17 a.m., I was standing in front of the mirror, playing over in my mind how my husband said he was afraid to tell me about his infidelity because he did not know if I would slap him or act out, and I just thought to myself, *He really doesn't know me at all,* and then the Holy Spirit said to me that we needed to date each other, start all over from scratch—nothing intimate, but to take time and really get to know each other from the beginning, the right way.

As I said before, God is a multitasker: while He was working on my marriage, He was also working on my husband and me individually. I needed to find out why correction and criticism felt so much like rejection to me, why I found my worth in accomplishments and seeking the approval of others, and why I let inconsiderate comments made by family members, friends, or people I had encountered throughout my life shape how I saw and thought of myself.

It is easy for parents or those closest to you to take out their pain and frustrations on you when they are hurting. Brokenness does not just happen; it builds up over time, chipping away at what a child thought she or he knew about herself or himself and forming something so warped and distorted that its tentacles are hard to unravel. As adults, we patch ourselves together with the lies the world feeds us about who we should be and what we should do instead of recognizing the hurt and pain and facing it so that we do not destroy the lives God places in our path.

Feeling favored was my haven; being cherished and poured into and loved unconditionally was my safe place. The problem

I now realize is that being favored did not fix the issues; they simply hid away and resurfaced as a desperate need to always please; no matter how it hurt or how much stress it put on me, I would never say no or want to disappoint for fear of falling out of favor.

There is a certain pressure and pain that come from being favored: you become a target. People would wait to see you fall so they could say, "I told you so," or there are expectations that you are expected to meet that come with a crushing heaviness.

Friend, we have a real enemy, whether we choose to believe it or not—an enemy who, in 1 Peter 5:8, we are told, "walks about like a roaring lion, seeking whom he may devour." The enemy wants to keep us from the healing and wholeness that God has for us because there is power in healing; there is victory when we are made whole. So, being favored by God makes us a target of the enemy because he knows the closer we get to God, the closer we get to walking in the plans and purposes God has for us, the closer Jesus's kingdom advances.

I would look in the mirror and see all the negative or hurtful things I was told about myself over the years instead of that I was created in the image of God and that He makes no mistakes. God wanted to pick apart and bring to the surface all these comments and lies that I had stored away, holding onto them, pulling them out like a reminder that I was not worthy, I was not good enough.

One day, many years ago, when I was about eighteen years old, I was sitting in the airport with someone who I thought was close to me. She looked at me and said, "You know, you're not as pretty as people think..."

This same person said this very same thing to me three times over the course of our thirty-year acquaintance, and for whatever reason, it angered me, but it also stayed with me.

Oftentimes we do not realize that there are spirits (evil ones) operating behind the people in our lives or people we meet. They know what plans God has for us, and the attacks begin early on to thwart us and stop us from our destiny. Some attacks may seem small such as the comment made to me all those years ago, and we may miss them, but they chip away at our self-esteem and self-worth, causing an abundance of other issues that create lasting problems in our lives. It may cause you to choose the wrong guy because you feel you cannot do any better or take a job you really don't want because the one you do want you don't think you're good enough or capable to go for. When the enemy makes a move, God already has another counter move in place. A year prior (and I only recall this recently), at seventeen years old, a little Jewish lady stared at me for quite some time as we both waited at the mall for our city buses to arrive. When her bus pulled up, she got up and came toward me, and she took my face in her tiny hands and said, "You are such a beautiful girl! A beautiful girl with such pretty eyes!" and she kissed me on the cheek. I was a bit embarrassed by the attention but thanked her before she boarded the bus, and I never saw her again. She may not have known it, but God used her to speak to that little girl who would need to draw on those words one day. This journey for me is going to be long!

August 20, 2021

What is wrong with me that I would rather sacrifice myself to hurt and pain than see someone who I love or care about (even if they've hurt me) go through hurt? And why am I having such a difficult time saying and knowing what I really want?

I've settled for so long and done without for so long that I have no idea what I want, let alone know how to ask for it. It could be because of how I was raised; we did not air our business and did not talk too much about our feelings. I can remember the first time I was able to have one of those honest conversations with my dad. Something had happened in our family, and sides were taken, and I felt alone, abandoned, and hurt. I built up the courage to verbalize how hurt I was...I was in my forties! My dad was not only receptive to the conversation but was also loving and comforting.

There's a certain rejection that comes when someone you care so deeply about feels as though you've let them down or you somehow feel you have disappointed them. It creates a feeling of being unwanted, alone, and broken. The burden of human favor is the fear of falling out of favor and disappointing the other person, so you are always eager to please and say yes, even when it hurts.

It was the same thing in my marriage: I did not know how to verbalize what I wanted, so I sacrificed my feelings and needs for years. It's the scars that people cannot see that cut the deepest—the devasting things that happen to us and keep us up at night.

August 21, 2021

God's Word in Psalm 30:5 (ESV) says, "For his anger is but for a moment, and his favor is for a lifetime." God's displeasure with our behaviors or actions is temporary and is meant to correct and discipline us, but His grace and acceptance are always with us. His favor is not something that is given and taken back each time we fall short.

As I pass through this season of trouble, I know the Lord is close to me, shielding and protecting me, lifting me up, and giving me strength for the battle because there is a certain peace that I cannot explain and a determination that can only come from the Lord. His Word says in 2 Corinthians 4:17–18,

> For our light affliction, which is but for a moment, is working for us a far more exceeding and eternal weight of glory, while we do not look at the things which are seen, but at the things which are not seen. For the things which are seen are temporary, but the things which are not seen are eternal.

Our afflictions or trials yield glory, but the glory comes in large part through the afflictions we experience. Our trials and troubles are but for a season compared to the glory we receive once tested, and we come out on the other side, having stood firm and steadfast in the Lord. As crushing a flower yields a sweet aroma, so the pressing that we experience strengthens our faith and trust in God.

As believers, we must not focus on what we see with our fleshly eyes but on what God is doing in us and for us, which is far greater than what we may go through temporarily. This is that comfort and peace that comes with trusting in the One who holds our lives in the palm of His hand, and His thoughts toward you are never to harm you but to give you hope and a future (Jeremiah 29:11). Whatever it is you're going through, the eternal glory that is to come out of it all is more precious than your carnal mind can ever imagine.

I cling to the fact that I know God is going to use this to bless, refine, and restore me, and in that, I rejoice. He will never allow anything to happen to me that would destroy me, so I know that this temporary affliction will be used for my good. There is a peace I feel deep down in my soul that no matter what confessions come or buried secrets are revealed, I will not be shaken because He hides me in His secret place and shelters me under His wings. There is no love as the love God has for His children: there is no wall He won't tear down, no chain He won't break, no mountain He won't move for us.

So, when a daughter of the King hurts, He comforts her, wraps His loving arms around her, and fills her with a peace that the human mind cannot comprehend. I am here to tell you: no matter what challenges you may face, no matter what you may be going through, if you trust in the Lord and truly open your heart to Him, He will tear down the gates of hell for you!

Trust in Him: His promises are real, and they are true. Something that years ago would have destroyed me, the Lord has turned me from mourning into dancing (Psalm 30:11) because what the enemy meant for my destruction, the Lord is working out for my good! Strength and fortification come with going through trials and challenges. You will never build endurance if you have never gone through strength training.

August 22, 2021

8 a.m.

I keep waking up early every day. At first, I thought that it was happening because my husband snores so horribly or that I couldn't sleep because I had so much on my mind that I just couldn't stay asleep, but I've realized that God wants time with me, quiet time spent in His presence. This quiet time is for me, time to feel His love filling me up. I need to quiet myself and spend time with God so that He can renew and restore me.

God protects, always cares for us, and guides us. Our total dependence on God likens us to sheep because we can do nothing without Him (John 10:11). We have nothing to fear (Philippians 4:19).

God speaks to us in so many ways—if we would only choose to listen. A Bible passage read by a pastor, a daily devotional reading, a prayer, or teaching that pops up on your YouTube account—He speaks!

A few days ago, God gave me the word "restoration" in the midst of this marital crisis I'm in that went off like an atomic bomb. At first, I thought it might be about my marriage, then thought it was about me, but today I realize it has many meanings and applications. The God we serve can do *all* things at *all* times. God can multitask.

The prayer I am listening to, from a channel I am not subscribed to, just popped up, talking about Psalm 23, and I came across the word "restore" again. I looked up the word online and found that it is applied in many ways and situations. "Restoration" means to "return something back to its original condition." The biblical definition of the word "restoration" is "to receive back more than has been lost to the point where the final state is greater than the original condition."[2]

The main point is that someone or something is improved beyond measure. At 8:36 a.m., God told me that this is why He woke me up—to tell me this very thing!

Unlike a traditional dictionary's definition of the word "restoration," the biblical meaning of the word has a much greater and deeper meaning that far exceeds (exceedingly and abundantly, above all we can ask, think, or imagine) what we think the word means or what we expect. God blesses the faithful; He blesses those of us who are His for standing steadfast in faith as we go through testing and trouble by paying us back double and giving us more than what we had before. He is not a God of "just enough"; there isn't anything God cannot do! God can breathe life into or restore any dead thing or situation. He breathed life into dust and created man, after all. Jesus swallowed death and spat it back out to save His sheep.

God may not always annihilate our enemies (which He absolutely has the power to do!), but He will make us victorious in their presence. God's promises are real, and they are true; God promised this to me, so I fully trust in Him and Him alone. In Psalm 23, the word "surely" means it is assured for those who follow Christ.

August 24, 2021

Last night was absolutely awful. I cried off and on through-out the night. I don't know if it was that I was watching *Say Yes to the Dress* or because this whole mess was taking me back to therapy, but the weight of everything just came down on me all at once, and I felt so overwhelmed that I thought my heart and mind would go off like a lit powder keg.

Then this immense feeling of nausea came over me, along with heat and awful pain in my shoulders. I had to take some-thing to help me sleep. I woke up this morning, and while the sick feeling was gone, sadness came over me like a funeral pall. I cried to God that my husband had not once asked me how I was doing in all of this destruction.

And just as God's Word says in Psalm 34:17, He is ever true to His word that "the righteous cry out, and the LORD hears and delivers them out of all their troubles" because my husband said, "Good morning," and then asked me how I was doing.

God is truly amazing! Do you see how quickly God will sometimes respond when we but ask? There is power in prayer.

Philippians 4:6–7 says,

Be anxious for nothing, but in everything by prayer and supplication, with thanksgiving, let your requests be made known to God; and the peace of God, which surpasses all understanding, will guard your hearts and minds through Christ Jesus.

When we go to God in prayer and give all our worries and cares over to Him, we can rest assured that He will take care of us—not that we will not have stress or worries, but that when we are faced with trouble, He will deliver us from it.

My husband and I had a good talk. I admitted that I should have never married him and should have walked away, but I regretted saying something that could be construed as callous and hurtful. He realized that he:

1. lacks compassion,
2. has an issue with women,
3. struggles with correction,
4. likes to be in control and have power,
5. feels abandoned by important women in his life,
6. holds grudges.

Without God, we continue to struggle with things that have happened to us in life or things that have been done to us. When we have a relationship with Jesus and allow God into our lives, into all the broken places, that is when we are set free. The enemy wants us to hold onto these shattered pieces of ourselves because it is all the harder to put them back together and we are robbed of a full life. Bitterness and pain fester when ignored, and these are the things that stand between God and us. Going before the throne and laying our burdens down removes the weight from our shoulders that we were never meant to carry. Jesus took all of this to the cross and conquered death so that we could live...live life more abundantly (John 10:10).

If the voices in our heads and the voices from the world are louder than that of God in our lives, we cannot walk in the plans and purposes that God has for our lives. We need to shut out the other voices and focus on what the Holy Spirit is saying to us and through those around us. Let God's voice be the loudest one in your head.

August 26, 2021

This morning, for the first time, I realized why God has me in the season I am currently in: this dry place, this desert, this season of great pressure. He needs to purge me of old beliefs, hurts, and insecurities that have been so deeply buried that only through the Holy Spirit have I been able to recognize and face this half-a-century-old demon. I cannot go into what He is calling me to, wanting to physically beat up anyone who attacks me and to argue with someone falsely accusing me of something because of my need to have everyone who matters to me see me a certain way or like me.

God, our loving Father, has a beautiful way of multitasking! My husband's infidelity exposed my hidden insecurities that not only played out in the sad drama but had tentacles stretching back to when I was four years old. It is amazing, when you look at a situation through spiritual eyes, how puzzle pieces begin to fit together, and the picture becomes clearer. Strange and random pieces spanning decades now paint a clear picture. That I, too, needed to face issues of the flesh, such as resentment, pride, spite, and the need for vengeance.

My going to therapy, despite going into it bitterly and grudg-ingly, will allow God to heal me in a multifaceted way, which will not only lead me down the path of marital restoration but also heal me in all my broken places from childhood to adoles-cence to adulthood. God is an awesome wonder-working God!

August 29, 2021

Infidelity

I haven't been sleeping well these past few nights and thought that God might want me in His presence. I believe that was true during the first few nights, but I think the other nights were me allowing my thoughts to take control.

I asked God, "How do I get through this mess? How do I navigate this unfamiliar space?" Infidelity is something that no one plans for, and while we can all decisively say what we would and would not do if we were in that situation, I am here to tell you that it is false. Sure, if you are walking in your flesh, it is easy to act on impulse and give in to your feelings, but when God's hand isn't in it, you must deal with the fallout. But friend, when God's hand is in it, nothing, to our logical minds, makes sense, but I have every trust in Him, my Father, my everything. So, when I asked God how to get through this, He said, "One step at a time." Not steps the way we see them with our carnal minds, but remember Psalm 37:23 says that "the steps of a good man are ordered by the LORD, and He delights in his way," meaning that God is in control of every aspect of those who act in accord with God's divine laws and that God delights in the course of his or her life. Following God's divine plan is sure to result in good outcomes for the obedient.

God told me to:

Step 1: trust in Him (Proverbs 3:5–6) and let Him have His way.

Step 2: go to counseling, be open, lay myself bare, be honest, and it is He who will dredge up what I need to face or resolve, and He will work it out for my good.

Step 3: be obedient. Whatever He is asking me to do during this season of my life, no matter what my rational mind thinks, being obedient (1 Samuel 15:22–23) is the key to healing and wholeness (Genesis 22:18, Romans 12:1).

God is a multitasking God. He can take one thing and have you work on it, and that single issue can fix many different things in your life. This season of crushing is a season of healing that will yield a fruitful harvest. Praise God! Thank You, Jesus!

August 30, 2021

Today started out as a good day because I was able to spend time with my son. I had a rough night because I felt as if I was lost and did not understand what my path was and that I didn't really know Scripture as I thought I did. The enemy was busy rummaging around in my head and building up lies as he always does.

When we're weak or tired, the enemy takes that as the perfect opportunity to sow confusion and get us to believe lies that draw us away from the truth of God's Word. When we have doubts, we should seek first the kingdom, meaning—seek out the guidance of the Holy Spirit and remember God's Word that says the enemy comes to kill, steal, and destroy: destroy our happiness, destroy our peace of mind, destroy our lives with whispered lies.

I have realized that one of the keys to a breakthrough is obedience. Being obedient means following what God is asking of us and allowing the Holy Spirit to lead and guide us. Sometimes we are in a rush to get the painful stuff over with or gloss over whatever we've gone through and pretend that it didn't happen, but the work that God wants us to do takes us through the pain.

I have had a strong urge not to do therapy because it's hard, but no matter what, I know it's an absolute must. This is how the enemy works: he attacks our minds and discourages us from doing the very thing, the difficult thing, that God needs us to do to work along with Him toward our restoration. The only way forward is *through*, and unless we are willing to do the work, there is no way for us to overcome the hurdles we face in life. There is no going back for us, no going back to the way things used to be.

Today was a rough day. I know God can do anything, and I know that when we get off course, God has ways of warning us of what could happen if we allow things to get off course. I wonder if I have the stamina to do all this: to do all that God is calling me to do and to do the work required to handle the challenges that come my way. Then I remember God's Word and promises in Proverbs 31:25, "Strength and honor are her clothing; she shall rejoice in time to come." We should know that we are worthy of honor and respect; we should settle into the peace that God has for us, and we can laugh at the future and whatever it may bring because our future is in God's mighty hand.

Here are a few other scriptures that I have found amazingly helpful: Romans 5:15, 1 Thessalonians 5:11, John 16:33, Psalm 121:1–2, Nehemiah 8:10, Isaiah 41:10, Exodus 15:2, Joshua 1:9, Isaiah 12:2, Isaiah 40:29, 1 Peter 5:10, Psalm 73:26, Philippians 4:13, 2 Corinthians 12:10, 2 Thessalonians 3:3, 1 Chronicles 16:11, 1 Corinthians 16:13, Habakkuk 3:19, Ephesians 6:10, Psalm 29:11, Deuteronomy 31:6, Psalm 27:1, Isaiah 40:31, Psalm 46:1–3.

Reminding yourself of the promises in the Word of God is like a balm or salve to the deep wounds we get along life's journey.

I know that I am, in this journey, neither alone nor power-less because I am in the loving arms of the Almighty and that Christ is my strength and my portion.

August 31, 2021

I went to see the doctor today and, on my way there, turned on one of my favorite programs on SiriusXM just in time to hear a woman give her testimony about how God kept her and surrounded her during the toughest moments in her life. This testimony really resonated with me because of what I am going through right now.

I know that Jehovah Jireh, the God who provides, has His loving arms wrapped around me. No matter what I am going through, I know that when I pass through the waters, God will be with me: "And through the rivers, they shall not overflow me. When I walk through the fire, I shall not be burned. Nor shall the flame scorch me" because God's Word says so in Isaiah 43:2 (paraphrased).

When God promises a thing, it is a certainty and will come to pass. He says in Isaiah 55:11, "So shall My word be that goes forth from My mouth; It shall not return to Me void, But it shall accomplish what I please, And it shall prosper in the thing for which I sent it." So, we should rejoice in our dry seasons, in our testing and troubles, because we know that God is urging us to listen to Him and heed His Word because all of God's promises will come to pass at His chosen time.

September 1, 2021

My Cup Runneth Over

Today was an odd sort of day. Situations happened at home where attitudes were high, and it really bothered me. I noticed that I allow other people's moods and behaviors to affect my mood in a negative way.

In the midst of this current storm, my daughter and sons are also going through turbulent waters of their own. It's hard watching your children go through painful situations, and all I want to do as a mother is fix it. But what do you do when a fix is not within your power? When there is nothing you can do but love them and be there for them during your own pain? I push aside my own pain and try to counsel and support my children as best as I can.

What comes to mind is the flight attendant on an aircraft: when they go through the emergency drills, they tell adult passengers on a plane to put their oxygen masks on first and then put the mask on the child because they would be no good to the child who is depending on them if they were to pass out.

How could I be of any use to those around me who are depending on me if I don't address the issues I am currently facing? I don't know how I got here, in this tumultuous place in my life, where everything that I knew to be true is a lie. It's like noticing the cracks in a wall for the first time and realizing that at any given moment, the wall can come crashing down.

I know that God is the one driving this entire thing, and I am trying to follow His plan during this season of my life, and while I know that God has me in the palm of His hands, I still find myself overwhelmed, wondering if I should be acting normal as my husband does—as if nothing has happened or it's behind us.

These are the struggles we face when we become lax in a situation and don't do the work that God sets before us. Yes, God can move mountains on our behalf, but we need to move the pebbles that cause us to stumble along the way. We must be working diligently toward the goalpost that God sets before us.

I know that I must be careful not to become complacent and go back to what is comfortable or easy because it won't fix the issues in our marriage whether we deal with it now or ten years from now. I'm also reminded of Psalm 46:10: "Be still, and know that I am God, I will be exalted among the nations, I will be exalted in the earth." This means that we are to stop meddling in areas that are strictly God's domain, such as changing other people, and do the work that He calls us to do, acknowledge our own faults, realize the things we must do to initiate change (being less critical, spending more time in God's presence), and allow the Holy Spirit to do a work in us. God is the One who delivers us.

Psalm 46:10 tells us to stop fighting in our own strength and allow Jesus to be our Savior and set us free. God is greater than any problem or situation that I could ever find myself in. I need to stop fighting in my own futile efforts—that's what is wearing me out—because I am looking at the big picture, thinking these are all things that I need to fix, but we must surrender to God's sovereignty, His faithfulness never to leave or forsake us, His omnipotence and unfailing love because all these areas are God's domain. Loosening our grip on control is what sets us on the path to deliverance because only God can bring us out of any situation. We should honor and exalt God; His power is truly unmatched!

What a comfort it is to know that we need not fret or worry because God has it all covered. So, in this season, I will be still and follow God's divine plan and guidance.

We need to trust God by giving all our cares and worries over into His capable hands and leaving all the details to Him.

I just feel that there is so much in my cup that it truly runs over, but I know that what the enemy meant for evil, God means for good (Genesis 59:29). So, this crushing and pressing that I know God will make sure yields sweet fruit. It is as if I am this tiny little girl holding tight to my powerful Father's hand as ominous waves threaten, and He bends low to whisper in my ear, "Don't be afraid; I've got you and won't let you go," and we both step into the deep void together, and as we move through the treacherous waters, a brilliant light shines and lights the way. What seemed scary and daunting and uncertain seems like nothing compared to the might and power of the One whose hands I'm in.

September 5, 2021

Criticism

"Criticism" is defined as "the act of passing judgment as to the merits of anything; the act of passing severe judgment, censure, faultfinding."[3] I have realized that criticism and how I process it have been a part of my life since I was a child—two diametrically opposed sides to my psyche: on the one hand, I was made to feel special and that I could conquer the world, and on the other, I was also made to feel I was no one special, and efforts were made to ensure I knew it. The negative reinforcement overruled any positive I received, making me feel unworthy. I now understand why I accepted staying in situations where I didn't feel loved, cherished, appreciated, or cared about, accepted subpar standards when God had His best waiting for me. That feeling of unworthiness followed me throughout my life like a stench. Feeling you are not worth the effort makes you blind to the truth, and you store away the pain and hurt to keep the lie going. The lie that you don't deserve better, that you have to accept things as they are, is a lie from the enemy, meant to keep us stuck.

Nevertheless, I know that God will get me through it. He has always been there, protecting me, guiding me, and opening and closing doors for me, whether I realized it or not. When we don't recognize our brokenness and have no idea who we are, we look to others to fill a void in our lives. We look to others to give us that thing that we cannot identify but feel we so desperately need, so desperately that we overlook the things in others that bring an even unhealthier component to our lives.

My husband had issues of his own that I masked over and ignored because I needed him to be someone who, in reality, he was not. I realize today that I expected the same perceived perfection from my children, not because I wanted to show off but because I didn't want anyone to criticize them, as it felt to me like a continuation of what I experienced growing up, and I didn't want that for them.

September 5, 2021

I listened to a sermon today that spoke about how our life experiences shape us and can oftentimes make you become someone hard and something you were never meant to be to survive the difficult and sometimes disastrous situations of your life, but you should instead declare that you will become all that God has created you to be.

For so long, I have morphed into someone I am not, allowing circumstances, people, or situations to dictate who I was at any given point in my life. It's time for me to be who God wants me to be so that I can walk into my promised land. This has been a season of struggle, strategy, the sovereignty of God, and discovering who I am in Christ. You must be brave enough to ask God to show you the real you, show you your faults, expose the wrong thinking, show you the areas where you need work, the parts of you that aren't really you but are things you've collected along the way and put on like borrowed clothes that do not fit.

Scripture says we are overcomers because Christ conquered death, hell, and the grave; because we are in Christ, we are, therefore, overcomers. In Greek, the word "overcome" is translated to *nikáō* (pronounced [nik-ah'-o]), which could also be translated as "to subdue, conquer, overcome, prevail, receive the victory."[4] This means that Jesus has already given us the power to defeat whatever situation we may be facing, subdue any enemy coming against us (being armed and equipped with Scripture), and prevail against any attack. God honors those who are faithful to Him and who diligently seek to grow spiritually despite the trials and struggles they may face. His Word promises, "Blessed is the man who remains steadfast under trial, for when he has stood the test he will receive the crown of life, which God has promised to those who love him" (James 1:12, ESV).

Here are a few more promises that should inspire and lift you up:

"Little children, you are from God and have overcome them, for he who is in you is greater than he who is in the world" (1 John 4:4, ESV).

"The one who conquers, I will grant him to sit with me on my throne, as I also conquered and sat down with my Father on his throne" (Revelation 3:21, ESV).

"The one who conquers will be clothed thus in white garments, and I will never blot his name out of the book of life. I will confess his name before my Father and before his angels" (Revelation 3:5, ESV).

"The one who conquers will have this heritage, and I will be his God and he will be my son" (Revelation 21:7, ESV).

"The one who conquers and who keeps my works until the end, to him I will give authority over the nations" (Revelation 2:26, ESV).

"He who has an ear, let him hear what the Spirit says to the churches. To the one who conquers I will grant to eat of the tree of life, which is in the paradise of God" (Revelation 2:7, ESV).

> The one who conquers, I will make him a pillar in the temple of my God. Never shall he go out of it, and I will write on him the name of my God, and the name of the city of my God, the new Jerusalem, which comes down from my God out of heaven, and my own new name.
>
> Revelation 3:12 (ESV)

September 7, 2021

What is at the heart of what I struggle with? Being a part of something for so long, for some reason, I've always felt as if I was on the outside looking in. Like on the precipice of life but not quite in the inner circle. Always feeling excluded in some way. In my mind, I didn't fit, so I immersed myself in other things: in books that took me away from reality where I could spin the story, I could be a part of, one where I fit. A world where I felt accepted and not different or "other than," where I felt loved unconditionally, and not that I could lose it when I made a mistake. I learned to fault others when I was the one who did something wrong because I was so afraid of making a misstep and losing the love that I did have. The consequence of accepting blame seemed dire, and, at a very young age, that meant losing everything.

People said they loved me, and most showed their love, but why did I feel so out of place and on rocky ground? I had trouble figuring out where I fit in and felt that I was on the outside looking in. I believe this is because we expect things from human beings that only God can give us. I learned to accept that

I was different and masked it by further setting myself apart. If the crowd went left, I had to go right. Everyone else wanted to be a part of a clique; I chose smaller, less-known circles of influence or friends. I managed to create a narrative, though untrue, that I was unworthy and just needed to take whatever I got. In my teens, I met some who pretended to be a friend but who would exploit my naivety and my feeling of unworthiness, and as I matured, it made me feel like a fool to have trusted such a person. When I look back, I see that it was as if I had a desperate need or desire to prove to those who, in my mind, wronged me or counted me out that I was and am worthy. I am not sure when or how my feelings and how I viewed myself became so distorted, but what God wants is to unravel the lies. Amid the chaos, God is putting order to things and renewing my mind in the process.

September 8, 2021

Today was a rough day: I got up late to find out that a colleague had quit, effective immediately. All day was spent working on things that he left hanging. I felt overwhelmed, extra annoyed, and overstimulated. So, it was a bad idea to surf social media because what the enemy does when we are tired or stressed is to find ways to attack our minds. Attack what we think and how we feel by showing us just how awful our lives supposedly are. Making us believe that we missed out or that our lives aren't up to par. This is why it's so important for us to remind ourselves of what God has promised us in His Word.

Peter Jackson did a fantastic job portraying J. R. R. Tolkien's character Gollum in his *The Lord of the Rings* trilogy. The audience witnesses Sméagol, whose journey began as a Stoor Hobbit, corrupted by the power and lure of the ring that his brother Déagol found in a riverbed. Sméagol's fall begins when he covets the ring so much that he kills his brother Déagol to get it.

The evil and darkness of the ring corrupt Sméagol, and we watch him transform into a twisted creature called Gollum as he gives himself over to the power of the "precious," as he calls it. Throughout the three movies, we watch the scenes with Gollum where he battles with himself as he plots and schemes his way through trying to get back the ring he'd lost while helping Frodo and Sam reach their goal of destroying the very thing he covets.

These scenes remind me of how our flesh battles each day against our spirit, each wanting different things—one ultimately leading to death and the other—life. This is what the apostle Paul talks about in Galatians 5:24 when he says that we must put to death our fleshly desires and commit our sinful propensities to God's control daily. God desires to have influence over every area of our lives (Galatians 5:25), not to control us, but for us to live abundant lives and be a true reflection of Jesus to the world.

September 9, 2021

The Holy Spirit reminded me that here I am, feeling sorry for myself and forgetting the promises that God has made in His Word: to never forsake us (Deuteronomy 31:8) and is able to do exceedingly and abundantly above all what we ask or think, according to the power that worketh within us (Ephesians 3:20). We must ask ourselves again, "Is He still not God?" We need to remind ourselves that God is accountable to His Word and that everything He has promised, He will fulfill. Once we grasp the idea that only God can give us true unconditional love, healing, and wholeness, we can put our expectations where they belong—in God. "But seek first the kingdom of God and His righteousness, and all of these things shall be added to you" (Matthew 6:33), meaning that we should seek God in prayer and that everything that we need or could imagine asking for, God will provide. So, instead of dwelling on what we didn't get as a child or what we weren't afforded in our lives, we should take it to the Lord and lay our burdens down. We shouldn't limit God by thinking small and expecting small, by only expecting what we can see with our eyes forgetting that we serve a supernatural, all-powerful God.

This journey is about discovering who I am in Christ. The me that God foreknew before He formed me in my mother's womb, not this broken me that cracked under a weight I was never meant to carry because we live in a fallen world. But God is able to do extraordinary miracles far beyond anything we can imagine, and when we put our trust in Him first and prioritize our Father's business, He will make all things come together.

September 13, 2021

Today, as soon as I woke up, I felt as though everything was coming apart at the seams. It didn't help that I was annoyed at someone else for not doing what they said they would do for me; then, I had to go take care of family business at the bank, which meant taking time from my workday, which usually made things hectic. All this pressure created such annoyance and frustration in me that I felt if one more thing was asked of me, I would explode. Then, I went to log into my work computer, and of course, the Microsoft Authenticator wasn't working, no matter what I tried. By this time, I was completely frustrated, and it was only 9 a.m.

I hardly spoke to my family, though I said "good morning" when I came home, but I must admit I was still miffed at one of my family members because I felt that the person could be selfish and rude at times. I felt that I was holding onto a grudge, and it felt wrong, and it felt wrong for a good reason. We are supposed to forgive just as God in Christ forgave us (Ephesians 4:32), but somehow, I managed to allow my flesh to have control and held on to the slight and allowed it to fester, causing me to be in a mood. These are the kinds of behaviors that hinder spiritual growth. The type of testing that strengthens our faith and helps us to grow up spiritually so that we are not tossed to and fro by our feelings. I failed at this completely today! How are our prayers to be heard if we stand praying yet hold slights against others or hold onto the pain of unforgiveness? Scripture says, "Whenever you stand praying, forgive, if you have anything against anyone, so that your Father also who is in heaven may forgive you your trespasses" (Mark 11:25, ESV). If we do not want to hinder our prayers, we cannot go before the throne holding onto grudges, with unconfessed sin, or with a bad attitude or mindset. I prayed that God changes me from this type of mindset and behavior because while it feels good to the flesh to slight someone at the moment or to "get back at" another person, that is killing our spiritual new man and giving the reigns over to the old man.

September 15, 2021

I was doing my morning routine and listening to a worship song, and God reminded me of an incident that happened early in my walk. I was standing at my bathroom sink brushing my teeth and heard a voice say to me, "Look down." When I looked down at the ground next to my right foot, there was a huge spider. I was petrified because it looked like a brown recluse. I moved slowly so as not to scare it off because we have brown carpeting in our bedroom that if it got away, we would never find it. I came back with a can of wasp spray and sprayed it in the corner where the spider was, and it didn't move. I was so afraid that it wasn't dead and might skitter off that I grabbed my shoe and gave it a good whack to make sure that it was dead. As I did, what looked like millions (well, to me, at that moment, it might as well had been millions) of what looked like ants shot out from the spider and began crawling around. I realized that those were baby spiders and began frantically spraying them before they could get away. God reminded me that if He cared enough about something so small as a pregnant spider, telling me to look down at the moment I did so that I wouldn't be harmed or the spider wasn't able to spawn, how much more important are the bigger things that He wouldn't move heaven and earth to protect and bless my family and me? To answer my prayers? Even about things I don't even know I need. This is how God cares for His children and protects us even in what may seem the smallest of ways.

These past few weeks have been a basket full of pain, confusion, anguish, anxiety, and strange contentment, and through it all, God has kept me: that is where the contentment comes from. I see it clearly and see the spirit behind the situation, one that was meant to break me and distort my view of myself. We let the enemy spin a web of lies in our minds like a spider, clouding our thoughts and hindering our view of how things really are, seeing things the way God meant for us to do. Scripture says the enemy comes to steal (our peace and peace of mind), kill (crush our spirits and the dreams God gave us), and destroy (our lives and our relationship with God) (John 10:10), but Jesus came to put an end to all of that, to open our spiritual eyes so that we see all that God created us to be and see how much He loves us. When we place our trust in God, in His Word, He reveals the tricks and schemes of the enemy and doesn't allow us to fall victim to his tactics. Though the enemy is crafty and devious, he is no match for our God who breaks strongholds; but we must be in agreement with God and not the enemy.

I now realize that none of the broken, distorted thoughts I had about myself crafted by someone else's machinations are based on any truth at all. The enemy perceives us as a threat early on and uses others to attack and distort our thinking. I thank God for the relationship. Thank You, God, for renewing my mind! Having a relationship with God means spending time with Him, getting to know Him through His word, speaking to Him through prayer, and developing intimacy through pouring out our hearts to Him and, in return, listening quietly to what He wants from us and being obedient to give Him what He asks. I know that God can restore every year that the locust has eaten (Joel 2:25). He promised me restoration and not just of my marriage but in every broken and dry place in my life; He is a God who is able to do exceedingly, abundantly, above all we could ask, think, or imagine (Ephesians 3:20–21). I thank the Holy Spirit for pointing out every wrong thought I have cultivated about myself over the years and the bad habits or wrong ways I have developed around and because of those thoughts.

September 17, 2021

Last night, as I tossed and turned between restless sleep and awake, God flashed the picture before my eyes of me in my teens when I had done something to my appearance so that it was surprising to everyone else but me. That was me not feeling like I was good enough. I wasn't pretty enough, thin enough—just not enough. Back then, I focused so heavily on the things that I thought were flaws. I scarcely knew anything positive about myself. It had nothing to do with my parents, family, or upbringing; sometimes, no matter how much love and affection we show our children or how much we try to protect or shield them from pain, how they see themselves or their self-image can become distorted. We live in a fallen world, where outside influences or a thoughtless word uttered play a role in how we see ourselves if the world is the mirror instead of God.

There were many situations where someone would offer up a backhanded compliment or a criticism masked as a joke (such as "if it weren't for this or that, you wouldn't be pretty"). If we would only stop and think about the things we say and how they affect the person the words are directed at, we would have more discretion, consideration, and compassion. Or rather, if we thought about how we would feel if someone said those words to us, we would think twice about saying it. We must remember that God does not take it lightly when we mistreat others with our words or our deeds. God cares about how we treat others because it speaks to our character; how we treat others demonstrates the characteristics that we carry on the inside, whether hidden or obvious.

September 18, 2021

Yesterday was my therapy session, and I had such apprehension about doing it because I'd had a rough week and really needed a break from so much input that I just didn't want to at all! But canceling was not an option because I needed to be obedient to God.

My therapist confirmed what I was thinking (what I am sure God put on my heart): that I need to forgive (not forget) what was done and that we both need to leave past hurts in the past and move forward. We need to start completely over again! From ground zero, day one. We need to start dating again and really get to know each other.

I realize now that I have always been fearful of hearing what my faults and issues were because I'd always seen it as more things that were piled up on top of all the other things that were wrong with me, some I had no control over, which of course was a lie! Going back to the beginning of my "not enough" mentality and the belief that I am "unworthy" narrative was and still is a painful process; so old me chose to ignore it, hide it, bury it, leave the Band-Aid on it and forget that it was there. But we serve an awesome God who doesn't just allow us to stay broken or remain in the valley. He lifts our heads up, shows us what's keeping us back, and teaches us through His Word how to press on.

What these false beliefs caused was a monster that fed off of these insecurities that grew into something that had such control over my emotions that I could barely form a cohesive thought when asked a question as simple as "how do you feel?" I had spent so many years measuring my words before answering such questions because I was afraid that my own answers could open a floodgate to emotions and feelings that I wanted to remain sealed shut. A door that held all of my brokenness and deep hurts that no one could see. I was fearful of answering a question that could fire a bullet that would completely shatter my carefully crafted walls. So, I stayed silent in my proverbial corner, choking on unspoken words, collecting slights and hurts, and storing them in a powder keg of bitterness that I hid well. The problem with doing that most of my life is that I began to lose sight of the real me and morph into someone I didn't recognize. Almost like the real me was curled up into a ball inside of who I had become. When I began to learn how to let my voice be heard, it would sometimes be vengeful and cutting. Arrogance, pride, and justification made my mouth a dangerous weapon that was then doing some of the same damage to others.

Walking with God, I mean truly having a relationship with God, is an amazing place to be because God has a beautiful way of turning our gaze inward and shining a light on all of those decaying and festering wounds that we need to debride and heal from. How can we serve others in His kingdom and be set free if we are carrying a load we were never meant to carry? There would be no room for the amazing love, peace, and freedoms that come with being His—a true child of God.

September 19, 2021

God woke me up this morning and simply said, "Write, write." Last night my husband lay in bed watching TV, and he turned to me and wanted intimacy that I was in no way ready for, and my heart sank. I wondered if he was for real, if he was serious. It was as if he was saying, "Okay, back to what is important to me," and all I could say was, "What?" All I could manage was to hold his hand. I felt so broken inside that he was so insensitive to what I was dealing with inside. It made me wonder just how serious he's really taking this process and if he realizes how damaging it would be for us to fall back into familiar routines without allowing God to do His work in both of us! It could derail everything. I was so disappointed because it came across as incredibly selfish. I see now why it's so important to listen to and follow the voice of the Holy Spirit and not our flesh because our flesh and feelings lead us down a path that leads to heartache and pain that, if we heed God, can be avoided.

I was listening to a prayer on YouTube, and the lady spoke about how some tests are to strengthen our faith and to test us and are not always from the enemy. Like with Job, sometimes

God will allow us to be tested to see if we would trust Him to deliver and protect us or trust in our own tools and abilities. She referenced Proverbs 17:3. When metals are forged to make weapons or refined to derive precious metals, they go through an exacting process that requires a specific skill, considerable heat, and stress. When God refines His children, we often must experience crushing and stress as well. Psalm 66:10 also references how God refines us as silver is refined. We must remember that the battle is not ours; it belongs to the Lord, and whatever testing He allows is for our development and growth as Christians. All of these trials I am going through are refining me like silver, pressing out all of the impurities, and strengthening my faith so that I will lack nothing and can stand firmly when trouble comes.

James 1:2–4 tells us that we should "count it all joy" when we experience the different trials in life because such testing produces patience. Such suffering, conflicts, or trouble aren't pleasant, but we should be happy when we go through these experiences because God is strengthening us in such a way that we won't just be able to manage the stressful situations but stand firm when under pressure and not allow the enemy to tear down our defenses and breach our spiritual gates.

September 20, 2021

Today was a rough but manageable day! Why do I feel slighted when I'm wrong? When I feel upset, why can't I say that I am? I also feel responsible for making other people not feel uncomfortable. When we allow ourselves to be controlled by our feelings or emotions, we allow them to sit on the throne of our hearts where God should be. Feelings are fickle and flawed and should not be allowed a say in any area of our lives. Proverbs 28:26 warns us that walking in wisdom delivers us but trusting in our own minds makes us fools. Our trust in God leads to blessings. Walking wisely means understanding that our security can only come by trusting God, not relying on ourselves.

Jeremiah 17:9 also tells us that our hearts (refers to our minds, the source of our thinking, feelings, and actions) are deceitful above all things and beyond cure, meaning we live in a fallen world with flawed flesh, ruled by the prince of this world and allowing our flesh to control us is essentially giving control of our lives over to the prince of darkness. So, we must consciously fight against what our thoughts and feelings lie and tell us. Doing so always leads us down a path that draws us away from God's plans and purposes for our lives and interferes with our relationship with God. Wisdom is allowing the Holy Spirit to lead and guide us. We must constantly bring every thought into the captivity of Christ, meaning we must be conscious of what we're thinking about, examine them before they begin to get dramatically out of control, and shift our focus back to God choosing the peace that He has to offer. God's Word says, "Many are the afflictions [persecution, pains, distress] of the righteous, but the LORD delivers him out of them all" (Psalm 34:19; hereinafter, comments in brackets are mine).

To be delivered, we must stop those negative thoughts from spiraling and rest in the peace of knowing God will bring us out and set us free from whatever is threatening our peace of mind. It's hard when you're in the midst of a trying situation because the first thing we usually reach for is, "How does this make me feel?" When instead, it should be to ask the question, "God, what do I need to learn from this?" or change our mind-sets. No matter what, I know that God's got me and that the Holy Spirit will help me with my thinking. Ruminating about negative thoughts takes away our power and gives it over to the enemy.

So, instead of replaying conversations that didn't go well in our heads and zeroing in on the negative thoughts, we should pour our hearts to God, cry if we need to, and ask the Holy Spirit to help us. Cut off the oxygen to those negative thoughts so that they have no room to breathe and grow. What a comfort it is to be able to rest in the knowledge that whatever God is teaching me, I will learn: close the door on that episode, on the lies my feelings tell me, and not look back.

September 21, 2021

God told me that (while I was reading Psalm 71) the good work that He began in me, He shall complete. As the psalm states: What glory is there for God if people see me and my family fall at the hands of the enemy? They will see the hand of the God of our salvation on our lives! Our experiences and what I have been going through since being saved are a living testimony. I now understand why therapy was such an important part of the healing process for my husband and me to expose all of the things in our lives that brought us to this point in our relationship so that the healing could begin. Going through every painful detail is necessary so that when the enemy brings his accusations against us, they will no longer have any power. Though I feel as if every time I make progress, I get shoved and slammed all the way back, the Holy Spirit reminds me that we have the power through Christ to come roaring back. This reminds me of a scene that I love, with Wonder Woman in the *Justice League* movie, where she was hit and went flying back, but she slid back on one knee, steadying herself, smiled, and threw herself back into the fight.

My husband made another admission today that was like a punch to the gut. I know it's important for us to get everything out so that we can have resolution and healing, but I can't deny the pain I feel. Each time I try to move past it all, he comes at me, revealing something new, especially when the confession touches on my insecurities and highlights my self-doubt, putting it on center stage. Those words tried to worm their way back into the hurt places, the brokenness, and latch onto the "not good enough," "not worth it" false narrative. The latest confessions gave me the feeling like "here is more evidence that what you believed is true," which is a lie from the pit of hell.

When the enemy floods our minds with negative thoughts, God's Word is a powerful weapon against these lies. I know that both of us are going through the pain right now, but I can't help feeling that I have given so much and was handed heartbreak in return. There is comfort in knowing that God is close to the brokenhearted, and He knows every part of me that hurts. It should. It surprises us that when the enemy knows that we are close to a breakthrough, he knows exactly where to hit us. The Bible says in 1 Peter 5:8, "Be alert and of sober mind. Your enemy the devil prowls around like a roaring lion looking for someone to devour." Notice the key word in this scripture is "like," meaning "as though" or "as if" he is a roaring lion, but he is not, and he has no power, only the power we give him by giving in to our emotions and negative thoughts. He studies us, waiting for a window of opportunity to use something or someone against us to drag us back into his snare and trap us there. But Jesus conquered death and the grave; He overcame the world so that we could have an abundant life, not for us to let a defeated foe have his way and wreak havoc in our lives!

I know I must recognize the enemy's tactics; they are not new:

- Steal my hope, peace, and happiness
- Kill my joy, thirst, and hunger for God—my trust in Him
- Destroy my family, my reason for living, the trust I have in God's Word and promise.

But, as I said before, he is a defeated foe! Jesus said in John 16:33, "These things I have spoken to you, that in Me you may have peace. In the world you will have tribulation; but be of good cheer, I have overcome the world." Jesus is telling us that we must be confident and courageous when we put our trust in God, as only He can give us the peace that surpasses all understanding in the midst of life's pressures.

So, while this season of crushing doesn't feel good, I am content because I know that through the blood of Jesus, God will keep His promise and will not allow the "waters" to overtake me. God's Word says,

> When you pass through the waters, I will be with you; and when you pass through the rivers, they will not overtake you. When you walk through the fire, you will not be burned; the flames will not set you ablaze.
>
> Isaiah 43:2

So, there is no way the enemy will ever win! I have the victory through Jesus Christ! That should be our battle cry when the enemy attacks us and starts spewing his lies.

September 22, 2021

I had a conversation with a friend that caused her to tell me to be careful how I hear and that she needed to be careful what she said to me because of how I take things. I sent her a text and asked her opinion on a delicate subject, and she responded that she was reluctant to answer me for fear of how I might take it. Immediately the enemy went to work, and I began to spiral. Instead of taking it as correction, I saw it as me not getting it, that I was somehow defective because I wasn't learning or growing as a Christian. This is how the enemy tries to thwart God's plan for us because if he can get us to feed into how we feel instead of feeding ourselves with the truth in God's Word, he wins. None of what I was thinking or crying about was of God! That feeling of condemnation and defeat? None of that is of God because there is no condemnation in Christ. During my meltdown, God reminded me that there was nothing I could do to make Him love me any more or any less, that I cannot do works, I cannot work to earn His love, that He already loves me with awesome love. I am His! That's what He wants us to remember when our thoughts and feelings go down the rabbit hole and try to take us with them.

My friend called me back, and the conversation went nothing like what I had anxiously anticipated. I had allowed the enemy to worm himself into my head and allowed him to get me all worked up. All of that sobbing and squalling was me putting the cart before the horse and allowing the enemy to steal the stage and giving up ground to him. The enemy can only take from us what we give up. My mistake and my error were that I was leaning on my own understanding. Leaning away from our own ability to understand things and toward God's by accepting God's truth and following His will for our lives instead of doing things the way we have been in the past. It means trusting God even when we can't see the big picture or know any of the details.

September 23, 2021

I feel God's presence evermore in this current season that I am in. I can feel God leading me and teaching me. While I am writing, He will remind me of a scripture or tell me to go back to review it again to see how it coincides with what He's currently showing me. God's Word in Romans 1:13 says that He "would not have you ignorant": God equips us with spiritual knowledge so that we do not go about ignorant of the enemy's tactics and attacks and how we can sometimes sabotage ourselves, thereby giving aid to the enemy. God gives us the information and tips that we need to do whatever He calls us to do, and sometimes we don't have all the pieces to the puzzle, but it's in those times that God wants us to trust Him and draw closer to Him.

I have come completely to the end of myself; everything I thought I knew, I've realized I know nothing. All the plans and techniques or strategies I've trusted over the years are rendered useless. It's a beautiful thing; I've finally realized that I can do nothing without God. We are nothing without Christ, and what amazing comfort and peace (through every storm) comes from knowing whose hands I'm in! That the Creator of the universe has got me in the palm of His hands, will never leave or forsake me, and will never let me fall (Deuteronomy 31:6, Numbers 23:19, Joshua 1:5, Psalm 121:3–5).

September 24, 2021

No matter what it looks like, God is truly awesome and never ceases to amaze me. I am a child in awe of my amazing Father. Sometimes I find myself wallowing, feeling sorry for myself, dwelling on the different ways people have hurt me, the scars they left, and sometimes even seeing that they seemed to have moved on, built lives, seeming to enjoy the spoils of the chaos they wrought along the way in the lives of others. They seem to be winning; the key word here being "seem" ("giving the impression of"). When you are a child of God and trust in Him, nothing is ever what it seems when you are looking at things carnally. I was doing my Bible reading this morning, and the spirit of God was right there with me, giving me clarity and understanding. It is amazing how He sets things up for our benefit and when we quiet ourselves long enough, He will answer our questions and open up our understanding of His Word.

Yesterday I had a moment where what my husband had done plagued my mind, and I allowed my mind (for a moment) to dwell on how one of the people he was involved with wrecked my relationship and went about their business, living their lives and building happiness for themselves while I'm here dealing with the fallout of what happened nearly twenty years ago. But as I read Psalms 72 and 73 and God spoke to me, He made me realize that I was seeing things in the natural and allowing my feelings to influence what I was thinking, but my enemies who hurt me were not "winning," as God is good to the "pure in heart," and my focus should be on what He has set before me and not on those who have wronged me. We should not look at the past but rather look to the future.

September 26, 2021

I went to bed at about 2:30 a.m. this morning (foolish), and God still woke me up at 7:30 a.m. I did not feel tired, and I surely could not go back to sleep. God reminded me to go back to Psalm 73. Hebrews 10:23 says, "Let us hold onto the confession of our hope without wavering, since He who promised is faithful." Whatever God says in His Word is true; whatever He speaks to our hearts and promises us, we must hold fast to those promises because He is faithful to see them come to pass. I am amazed when I reflect on where I am in my walk right now and where God has brought me from: from being judgmental, easily angered, and annoyed; I cannot deny God's hand on my life and the work that the Holy Spirit has done in me. I forgave my husband right after he made his confession. That doesn't mean it didn't hurt me or didn't cut deeply, but that God was the orchestrator of every situation in my life, meaning that He's conducting the symphony even though He didn't always select the piece (some of our trials or attacks are orchestrated by the enemy, but God turns them around for our good), but not one instrument plays that He hasn't given permission, not one off-key note He won't use to make a beautiful concert piece. So, the parts of my story that may have destroyed me, had it not been for God, merely hurt but cannot destroy. Instead of doing what I've done in the past: storing up hurts, keeping a record of slights, allowing them to attach themselves to deeply rooted insecurities like parasites, and echoing lies that the enemy has told me most of my life, I've chosen to believe that Jesus died on the cross and that God sacrificed His one and only Son because He loves me, because I am worth it.

What do you do when the struggle isn't to forgive the person who wronged you but to forget what they've done, leave it in the past, and start over? I realized that I came to the "end of myself," the end of what I myself am able to do. In this situation, I had to hand the reigns over to God. Only He could put my feelings and emotions into words. Only He could tell me what I was thinking or feeling and why. Only He could heal me and tell me what to do because He knew me before He intentionally formed me in my mother's womb. God knows us better than we know ourselves, so when we let go and let the Master Conductor take control, we're able to do and let go of things we'd never imagined we could. Be still and know that He is God; rest in the comfort that you are in the hands of Abba, the One who spoke worlds into existence, who hung the moon and the stars, who tells the winds where to blow, the waters how far they can go, and who knows where the thunder is storing up! There are no better hands in which to be!

God's Word says in Psalm 37:38, "But the transgressors shall be destroyed together; the future of the wicked shall be cut off": God is not slack that He would ignore evil and what happens to those who are His; when we were still sinners, Jesus died for every one of us, so all had the chance to be saved. The wicked only seem to prosper, but they will enjoy success only for a time until it all comes to an end in God's perfect timing. So, no matter how things may seem in the moment, God is urging me not to dwell on past hurts. He's been strategically dredging them all up and bringing them front and center so that I could see that they have no basis or no power. To destroy the lies of the enemy and untangle the web of lies he's spun in my mind for forty-five years, I must go *through* it, not around, under, or over it, but through it so that Jesus can set me free from it once and for all. When we face the "Goliaths" in our lives, we take back a weapon the accuser of the brethren can use against us and add one more weapon to our belt of truth because we're standing on the only truth, and that is the Word of God!

This week I got a call from my brother to discuss the clean-up of a property that we all own. Lush green vegetation grew so high and so deep that you could no longer see there was a house in there somewhere. He took pictures along the way and video so we could see each step in the process; there was but a remnant of a driveway because the many coconut trees and other vegetation had completely covered everything. Within hours, the backhoe driver had the front of the property cleared. It revealed the burned-out structure that was once our childhood home, bringing back so many happy memories. Hidden by what appeared to be healthy greenery was a structure crumbling under the weight of what seemed good and healthy, which it was never meant to bear. The back of the property was worse than we had thought. The backhoe driver revealed once some of the vegetation was cleared away, the garbage and filth that neighbors, some of whom we knew and grew up with, had tossed their filth and refuse onto our property, costing us thousands of dollars to clear away.

One section that was being cleared tore down an entire exterior wall of the house, revealing fatal cracks in the structure, so we all came to the agreement that the house was no longer viable and needed to be torn down to its foundation. The question was then: Was the foundation sound and viable?

This story is like the lies the enemy plants in our minds, dumping toxic waste that, over time, we accept and believe. Those lies take root and form little cracks that change how we see things and ourselves, and we cover it all up with things we think are good, such as collecting worldly possessions, trusting the wrong people because our thinking is warped, taking on worries and stress to spare others the pain, believing we're not worthy because of the toxic waste we've allowed people to dump and heap upon us in secret. We cover up the cracks they cause, but the cracks become destructive, and soon, the weight of it all causes the walls we've built over time to crumble.

Walls that were poorly built on a foundation of lies. God is in control of the backhoe in this season of my life, tearing down and clearing away the vegetation that I've let grow over the hidden garbage and wreckage. God is exposing the burned-out shell, pushing aside the fond memories that I cherry-pick, and He makes me face the hard truths: What triggered my need to please? My fear of being abandoned. My desire to remain unseen for fear of being overlooked? My low self-value? Why I'm okay being the one hurting if it spares someone I care about from being hurt? Why the self-sacrifice? The belief that I am not worthy? God tore down the vegetation and exposed the waste so that He could tear down the walls of lies and repair and rebuild my foundation, my belief system. In this, all the turmoil, upheaval, and pain, I can rest in the comfort that, as I go through the pressing and the crushing, God is faithful to restore me and restore a relationship that seemed beyond repair. My heart is full of how much God loves us and cares for us, that He takes time to do things in our lives that we are incapable of doing on our own. He's giving me the strength to go through and deal with things I would have run from or hidden away in the past.

God is an awesome God! A good Father. He reminded me that my thoughts needed to be changed so that they line up with His current plans for me. That means praying and seeking the guidance of the Holy Spirit before saying something or acting on an impulse or taking charge of a situation when what God needs me to do is to be still and allow Him to work.

Jumping in and taking control of a situation and then complaining about the responsibility that falls on my shoulders is precisely the thing God is trying to prevent. We often make decisions that are not good for us, and when things don't work out the way we'd hoped, or they go horribly wrong, we question where God is amid it all, not realizing that when we take up the reigns and seize control; we are essentially telling God that we don't need His help. In these moments, we must be still and let God be God and trust that He is working all things out and that it will be good.

September 28, 2021

God is faithful and true to His word! He is not man that He should lie. If He said it, I know, trust, and believe He will do it. I listened to a sermon yesterday, and the message was to stop striving, meaning to stop trying to make things happen on your own and be still and know that He is God—all-powerful, all-knowing, able to do exceedingly and abundantly! God doesn't need our help to accomplish His plans; He needs us to be obedient. The Bible says He will give you houses you didn't build and vineyards you didn't plant! So, instead of worrying about how things will happen or whether they will be done, we need only to trust that, whatever God is doing, it will be for our good. However, if we want God to move, we too have a part to play in the process by being obedient and by doing the things God asks us to do; that means forgiving one another, reading His Word, praying, depending on Him, and not giving in to our own selfish needs or desires.

I see now how important it is to remind ourselves that we need God and how much we depend on Him to change us and do the work in us that we are not able to do on our own. Today my husband and I got into an argument because I called him niggardly, and he was offended. I said this because he can be very stingy and exact, wanting to know who is paying for what and tracking who paid for what last, as if we are dating as opposed to being married. I also find that he does things that he knows irritate me in a passive-aggressive way to get back at me. I get angry and then act on that anger. The Bible urges us to be angry but not to sin (Ephesians 4:26) because it is an open door for the enemy to come storming in and feed into our slighted feelings, causing strife in a relationship. I found myself going to God, asking Him to change my husband and remove those tendencies from him, but rather what my request should have been was for God to change me. There is nothing good in us, and if we are to grow as Christians, we must be honest with ourselves and recognize the habits and behaviors that we exhibit that are not pleasing to God and causing strife in our lives. We are sometimes the authors of our own tragedies, meaning some difficult times are brought on by our disobedience and reluctance to change. Scripture says in Proverbs 15:1 that "a gentle answer turns away wrath, but a harsh word stirs up anger." Think about how an argument starts and quickly escalates. Each person's ire rises, and they attack the other person, giving in to what feels good to our flesh: to get back at or to hurt the other person. Instead, answering calmly in a kind or peaceful way takes all the fuel out of the fire and causes us to view the situation from a spiritual view by asking ourselves who profits from you getting into an argument and saying things that are hurtful and cruel. This is where self-control comes in; this is all part of God's plan to restore. By rooting out the bad and damaging habits, there is room for the Holy Spirit to fill us with His fruits.

September 29, 2021

Yesterday was a struggle, not just for me but for my husband as well. I saw what happens when pressure or stress comes: we go to our separate corners and come out swinging. We forget what God's Word has taught us and fall back into selfish habits and a "poor me" mentality. I am thankful that I am in a place where I can step back and see the errors we are still committing. Friend, I must tell you that self-reflection is an important part of this process, and in all humility, asking ourselves how we are contributing to a negative situation and what we can consciously change to improve. I thank God for the extensive work He's done in me and the grace He's given me for the trials I am going through. I know God allows us to experience times of testing and troubles to purge us of all that is not pleasing to Him and to refine and perfect us to prepare us for the call He has on our lives.

I could not imagine having these petty, small-minded grievances when God takes me to the next level in my walk; it would be a destructive thing that would have the enemy lying in wait for the opportunity to try to undo all of the work God as done thus far. It is sometimes difficult when we are being corrected to hear what we are doing wrong, but it is necessary. I've come to realize that even those who hurt us and do wrong need to be loved and to know how much they, too, mean to God. That their mistakes don't have to define them, and they don't have to keep living with the guilt and shame of what they have done. If I decide to pray for and hope for God to restore my relationship, I will need to do my part as well. Just because I didn't do anything to deserve what was done to me does not mean that God doesn't need to bring things out of me that He wants to expose and correct. The way both of us hold grudges, hold onto slights, make snide remarks, or brood in silence when we don't get our way are all poison that rots and eats away at the foundation of any relationship and cannot go where God plans to take you.

September 30, 2021

Perceiving the Shift

Every time we pray and make supplications before the Lord, things are already happening in the spirit. When we pray, we have to believe that we've already received whatever we've prayed for. Even if we don't see things happening or changing, that does not mean that God isn't working on our behalf; it's our faith that defeats the enemy. First John 5:4 says, "For whatever is born of God overcomes the world. And this is the victory that has overcome the world—our faith," meaning no matter what stumbling blocks the enemy tries to place in our path to hinder us, our faith is what gives us the victory and strips the enemy of his power. Remember: his goal is to get us to turn away from God, but as long as we believe in Christ and trust God's Word, we have the victory.

October 1, 2021

God is faithful and true to His word even when we don't deserve it. Matthew 6:6 says that when God sees us praying in secret, He will bless us openly. Jesus teaches us that why we pray determines how we pray (verse 7)—*motives!*

I've been praying throughout this process for God to get me through this situation at this point and time in my life. Yesterday I had a session with my therapist, and she mentioned how amazed she is at how I've seemed to forgive my husband so quickly and self-reflect in such a healthy way, as she herself went through the same situation two times and still deals with anger toward her last husband years later. She mentioned how amazed she was that I came to her with the mindset of delving into what my own issues were that needed to be addressed next, while I knew I was not responsible for the situation that occurred, nor did I cause it. I needed to dig into how I got here and why I ignored obvious signs and stayed.

This is all God. God gave me the grace through the Holy Spirit to forgive my husband and let go of the transgression because there is a bigger picture here. Does it mean I will forget? No, it means I can deal with it and move on. There are times he may say something, and I may be taken back to what he did, but it doesn't consume me and take me back to that broken place. I had a newfound peace and approach to what lies ahead: this comes from acknowledging I can do nothing on my own, and to have true peace and healing, I had to relinquish control to God. God created each of us in His perfect wisdom and perfect plan; only He knows how our hearts and minds work; only He knows what we need and when. Giving all authority to God and following the Holy Spirit's lead is what got me here and will get me through. Do I sometimes fall short? Yes! Do I sometimes stumble and fall? Yes! The important thing is to get back up and try again. The Bible says in Proverbs 24:16, "For a righteous man may fall seven times and rise again, but the wicked shall fall by calamity." We cannot wallow in self-pity and allow ourselves to stay stuck because the trials that we face today are what strengthen us for the more complex tests that may come in the future. Psalm 37:24 says, "He shall not be utterly cast down; For the LORD upholds him with His hand." So, while I know I will sometimes stumble and fall, God will catch me by the hand and set me upright again. We are imperfect, and our Father knows this and is there with us through it all, lifting us up when we stumble. God picks us up, dusts us off, and gives us the courage to keep trying and the strength to push through. That's what a good father does: he supports his children financially, emotionally, and physically; how much more do you think our Heavenly Father loves and will support us? I am humbled that He walks with me, helping me to navigate this difficult time in my life and carrying me when I'm unable to do it on my own. I may not see the future, but I know good things lie ahead because I am in God's loving and mighty hand!

October 2, 2021

This morning we got up late and didn't have very much to do, so we went out to eat. My husband seemed distant; I don't know why, but I won't assume or get into my feelings about it because I didn't know why. If I wasn't going to ask what was wrong, I wasn't about to assume—that's growth!

Sometimes it's hard to self-reflect and face the things that broke you at key points in your life, but the key to a closer relationship with God is to remove any obstacles that take up time and space in our lives that usurp territory that should belong to God and God alone. Jesus died on the cross to restore our right to a personal and meaningful relationship with our Heavenly Father. Anything we remember or obsess over, overindulging, seems to occupy space in our minds and hearts that belong to Him. I've been on this journey for almost two months now and could not imagine walking this journey and weathering this season without God, the roadmap Jesus gave us, and the guidance of the Holy Spirit. There is a certainty that I will get through this, that things will be better, and that there is a great peace that comes when my burden is given over to God because

I no longer have to figure anything out or am not plagued by uncertainty because I know there is no better place to be than in the shelter of the Most High.

I listened to a sermon today that spoke about how the enemy attacks and that he attacks those with open doors, places where we are weakest or most insecure, and creeps in and wreaks havoc. The word "insecure" means "subject to fears, doubts, etc.; not confident or certain; uneasy; anxious"⁵—all based on lies from the enemy. What I know for sure:

Jesus's love is with an everlasting love (Jeremiah 31:3). Hope in the Lord brings security (Job 11:18). God tells us to be confident because it will be rewarded (Hebrews 10:35–36). This comes from trusting in Him completely. Jesus tells us to be anxious for nothing! (Philippians 4:6) that we should cast all our cares on the Lord. He knows what we need and will provide (Matthew 6:26).

So, in this season, the Holy Spirit is teaching me to continue doing what He is asking of me, to be obedient, and I am amazed at how, at each turn, it is clear there is a kind of peace, a kind of calm, a kind of contentment that cannot be explained in the natural. This is a peace that surpasses all human understanding and is clearly supernatural and all God! Yes, the thoughts come when we may watch a movie that depicts the thing that we struggle with or was done to us, or questions pop up when my husband reminisces about his time traveling for work; but they are quickly put in check by the Holy Spirit. I can ask a question, and while the answer may hurt at that moment, it doesn't consume me, and I don't obsess about it. I am able to self-reflect and see how a teaching or Bible lesson exposes something from my childhood or my past that takes me to a broken place. A place where I felt unworthy or "less than," but rather than stuff it away and ignore it, I can say, "There you are, now I understand," and can face it and allow God to heal and bind up that wounded part of me. Imagine: Jesus died on the cross once and for all; He died on the cross for me, for the world. Now I must learn to love myself and how to properly love others.

This past week was a bit emotional as I watched my childhood home being torn down to the foundation; all the happy memories we made there, growing up; yes, we had some tough times and situations I would rather forget; but it was the hallmark of my childhood—gone. But the reason was because the structure was no longer sound, just as the lies the enemy spoke to me and I believed needed to be exposed and torn down. We tore it down so we could rebuild a home, a more sound structure. Isn't that what restoration means? Restore the homestead, a renewal, a revival, a return to its original unimpaired condition. To be made new.

That is what God is doing in me, in my marriage, in my family. And He whispered to me, "Make new memories." Bless God!

October 3, 2021

I learned early on in my life not to take advice from anyone whose experiences were based on "I think," meaning they'd never gone through—because often a person's bitterness or jaded outlook or even their mood can color the advice they give you. We all are susceptible to such situations, and none are immune, which is why we should use wisdom and not give advice about things we know nothing about. For example, a married person should not be taking marriage advice from someone who has never been married. While God can give anyone a word for us, we must use wisdom when confiding in and seeking advice from anyone, especially from those who aren't truly saved.

We must be careful who we allow to influence us and speak into our lives as children of God. At this point in my life, I seek out God and am learning how to hear and heed His voice more. There have been times when God gives me a word, and it is confirmed through my devotion for the day or something a loved one might say in a conversation we're having, and I know in my spirit that God is giving me a word. I have finally realized how much I depend on and should depend on Him and only Him.

Even when I wasn't walking with God, it was He who kept bad situations from becoming disasters, He who opened doors of opportunity that elevated me, not my intelligence, but His. It is His Holy Spirit dwelling in us that draws people to us, to want to be around us, to hear what we have to say because it is the Spirit at work. When we stick with God, He can take us places we have never dreamed of.

I was reading John 7:6 and John 6:25–29 and the commentary that goes along with it. Jesus told His brothers, who told Him to go show Himself to the world so they could see the miracles He'd performed, that His time had not yet come, that they were free to do what they wanted, but He had a higher purpose. When God has a call upon your life, you cannot set your own goals or timelines because God's plans and purposes will prevail (Proverbs 19:21). Think about Abram when he was told by God to leave his entire family and the only life he knew behind him and sent him into a land he didn't know. Abram was obedient to God; he didn't know what to expect or what lay ahead for him but trusted God. No matter what things look like, no matter what pain we are feeling, no matter the struggle, we must trust God to bring us through it and believe that if God's allowed it, He will use it for our benefit. I know in my spirit that these trials that I am going through and the pain I sometimes feel, God is drawing me closer to Him and is strengthening me.

Sometimes it can be easy to get caught up in the pressures of the world, allowing the timeline the world has laid out to dictate to us, causing us to feel we are behind on some scale we measure ourselves by. For me, it was seeing others accomplishing, at a young age, the dream of becoming a writer/author, making me feel as though I was a failure, but in truth, God's timing is perfect, and nothing, I mean nothing, happens before it's time. With God, there is a time and purpose to everything.

At the beginning of this painful journey, the enemy told me staying in this relationship would make me weak, make me a fool, and it's all lies! The enemy wants me to launch too soon, meaning—to get out before God has a chance to turn things around and before He has a chance to do His work in me, to operate outside of God's plan and purpose (listening to the world). Instead of saying, "Poor me," we should be questioning, "What good thing God has on the other side of this Red Sea that the enemy does not want me to reach?" Remember, friend, the enemy wants us to fail, wants us to miss all that God has planned for us. That tells me the enemy is scared and is trying tactics that worked in the past. The enemy's attacks tell me that I'm on the right path, and the way he is ramping up his attacks means that what God has in store is even bigger than I could imagine. So, the question is: Who do you believe? Whose plan do you follow? For me, I will follow the One, the only One who, in John 10:28 (ESV), said, "I give them eternal life, and they will never perish, and no one will snatch them out of my hand." The Lord says in Isaiah 49:16 that our names are engraved on His palm and that God's thoughts are focused on the well-being of His people (Psalm 40:2)!

I can take all my worries and cares to my Father in heaven, and He will give me rest for my weary soul. He will order my steps and work out all the details with my best interest in mind. God loves us and wants only what's best for us, so I trust fully that the path He currently has me on, and though I may not see it (no matter what anyone says), He will work it all out for my benefit. I trust that He knows the end from the beginning and is refining and perfecting me so that when I get to where He's taking me, I am well prepared. The first steps in the right direction are submission (setting my wants and desires aside and giving all control to the Holy Spirit), obedience (doing whatever He leads me to do, whether that is to forgive, go to counseling, change behaviors), then leave the rest to God. God's Word says, "The Lord will withhold no good thing from those who do what is right" (Psalm 84:11).

October 4, 2021

Today at work, I really felt the pressure of being in a place where I do not belong. While I respect our new manager and her authority, I answer to a higher authority. I am reminded of God's plan for my life. When we start to feel the weight of our problems or issues, we need to go into fellowship with God. The word "fellowship" means, in Greek, "partnership, participation, or to communicate, communication, contribution, willing to communicate." According to *Merriam-Webster*, the word is *koinōnia*: "holding something in common."[6] It is a description of the intimate relationship that believers have with God through Jesus Christ. In some respects, it is similar to the partnership we see between God and people in the Old Testament. Covenant images clearly suggest a kind of fellowship between God and His people. As He did with people in the Bible:

- He "walked" with Enoch.
- He called Abraham His "friend."
- Moses talked with God "face-to-face."

All suggest a close and special bond, a relationship. Each of these relationships suggests that God desired a relationship with shared interests and common goals.

I am humbled and blown away by this amazing gift from God: that He thinks of each of us and wants to fellowship and be in a deep and intimate relationship with us. I don't know about you, but that makes my heart so full that He loves me so much that He wants to walk with me and talk with me and call me His friend! But we must remember that an intimate relationship requires friendship and close personal attachment. When I think of a marriage, this is its key component: two people in communion, sharing in a close relationship, sharing in common goals, participating, and sharing in a mutually beneficial relationship. Each with loving regard for the other.

Relationships must be nurtured, fed, and worked on. Jesus shows us throughout the Bible how to accomplish this. When I think about my relationship, I can see parallels to our relationship with God. What sower plants a seed and walks away from it? You have to water it, feed it nutrients, prune it when necessary, and care for it if you want it to bear fruit; otherwise, it withers and dies or doesn't grow at all. If not protected, harsh elements (sometimes outside or internal) or neglect can also cause the decay or deterioration of any relationship. Whatever we don't feed dies. Think of marriage this way:

- *outside* (harsh weather, infestation): interference or negative influence of others;
- *internal* (disease, lack of nutrients): inner conflict or turmoil, unresolved or unaddressed issues.

The answer to all of the above is God, reading His Word to see what a real relationship is, talking to Him through prayer, and being in communion with Him through prayer, worship, and praise.

I am so amazed by how God, out of billions of people on the earth, if we seek Him, will make time to speak to us. He works with each of us according to how He made us, so each person's walk will be different, just as we saw in the Bible with Enoch, Abraham, and Moses.

October 5, 2021

Much Fruit

I looked outside at the guava tree that my youngest son bought for me a year and a half ago as a Mother's Day gift. I marveled at how much good fruit she produced this season though she was beaten down and battered by the many awful rains and windstorms that threatened to uproot her, yet she held onto her blossoms and produced so much fragrant and sweet fruit that I didn't have room to consume, so we shared some with our neighbor. I was amazed at how she continued to bear fruit despite a small, seemingly frail trunk and branches that were splayed out wide instead of growing toward the sky because of the heavy rains. Nevertheless, we pruned the tree, and she continued to grow her branches full of thick greenery and beautiful large fruit.

When I think about my guava tree, I think about what we go through as believers. Only God knows what He's put deep down inside of us and what we are truly capable of. Only He knows what testing and trials we may face, but with a bit of pruning and care, we grow in Christ and produce the rich fruits of the Spirit. Though the storm may rage and batter us, the soil we are planted in matters because when we are planted in Christ, we can weather any storm and can bear fruit to the full. The word "bear," according to the *Merriam-Webster's Dictionary*, means "to support the weight of, to give birth to, to produce as yield, to permit growth of, to produce a desired result or reward."[7] In James 1:2–4, Scripture says we should assess the way we view the trials we face in life when we go through troubles and hardships because the testing of our faith produces steadfastness and that we should allow faithfulness to come to fruition so that we mature spiritually and can stand firm when the next trial or testing comes.

It is amazing how God can truly transform our minds and change our hearts once we allow ourselves to be filled with the Holy Spirit and let Jesus light our paths. There is a calm, a certain peace and contentment that cannot be explained because God's hand is guiding every area of my life; I know that the Holy Spirit is always giving me peace and calm that I would not normally have. Each day, changing me so that I no longer hold onto the hurt that could have been damaging to me when my husband confessed; but I no longer see the same. I thank God that "He who has begun a good work in you will complete it until the day of Jesus Christ" (Philippians 1:6) means that God will continue to work on and perfect me until the second coming of Christ.

I still do sometimes fall back into old irritable feelings, and behaviors still try to creep in and do, but thank God that the Holy Spirit continues to perfect and refine His work in me.

All honor and glory to God! The one who loves and blesses me. Read through Psalms 90 and 91 and reflect on the fact that when we are in covenant fellowship with God, all the hosts of heaven back us and cover us when we call on the Lord of hosts. I believe that when God's hand is on our lives, there is nothing any force from hell can do.

I remember that in 2002, I was rushing to my five-year-old daughter's ballet practice, and we were running late. I had my three-year-old son in the back seat next to his sister. I was probably going about eighty mph and coming up on a green light that quickly went from yellow to red. Rather than stop, as I knew I should, I floored it and blew through the red light. There was a black Trans Am coming up even faster on my right, and as we both blew through the red light, traffic came barreling into the intersection toward us from the left. I made it through the intersection but watched to my right as a minivan (that missed me) plowed into the Trans Am, causing it to disintegrate and sending pieces flying everywhere. I remembered feeling horribly for the person because it was a direct hit on the driver's side. I felt as if, had I obeyed the yellow light and slowed down in anticipation of the red light, he would have stopped as well. I was so thankful to God because I knew it had been His grace and His hand that protected the children and me when I was doing something so foolish and dangerous. I was not yet saved, and still, God protected us.

October 7, 2021

Today was an odd day; I felt the enemy trying to attack me like a pall sitting over the day. I found myself irritated by things and just in a down, irritated mood. I know for sure there are things God is trying to work out of me. This week I realized something that my husband still does that rankles me; when I'm talking to him about something, and I'm right, he dismisses me and turns to have the same conversation with our daughter, then she says the same thing, and he agrees with her as if I didn't just say the same thing prior. It annoyed me to no end and even more so because he said she explained it so he could understand. What in the world? She basically repeated what I said and agreed with me. Then I got annoyed with my daughter because she kept asking me if I was mad, and she kept on asking because my mood truly did change, but it was because my irritation turned to hurt because what I was saying to him was to help him because I noticed a physical change in him, indicating a health issue, and all he wanted to do was roll his eyes and dismiss me. I know this was me allowing my feelings to take charge, but I felt disrespected, but that's something I know I need to let the Lord dig up the roots of this hindrance to my spiritual growth and allow Him to heal those wounds up because they are rooted in that feeling of being "not good enough" or whatever it is I am dealing with at any given moment, whether it's a struggle with the need to be right, feeling slighted, or some other unimportant momentary thing that I need to be set free from. I am leaning on God and trusting that the Holy Spirit will help rid me of these insecurities that have no basis in truth at all and cleanse me. The enemy feeds us lies when we are at our most vulnerable and often goes back to lies that he's had us believing for most of our lives. The truth is that God loves me in spite of my faults and imperfections so much that He sent Jesus Christ to take my sins to the cross so that I could be close to Him. I am more than enough, no matter what lies the enemy speaks or what people may say; God does not make mistakes. I am fearfully and wonderfully made. Created exactly to God's specifications and made for such a time as this! Yes, more than enough, more than a conqueror through Christ who gives me strength. God calls me to what I was created for because He has uniquely qualified me, so everything He's called me to do, I am well-equipped to do.

October 8, 2021

Struggles

I've been met with another challenge, and I know God's hand is in it and using it to refine me. My husband has been sick since the middle of the week, and he finally went to the doctor on Thursday. He had first asked me to go with him as he always does, and it felt like he wanted a mother to hold his hand because he felt sick. Never mind that I had been giving him sound advice about his health, and he rudely dismissed me. Once he found out he had a sinus infection and needed to see an orthopedic for an arthritic issue in his shoulder, he began to cling to me and hug me the way a child would a parent when they are not feeling well; it made me feel uncomfortable and a bit irritated to be honest. Then the Holy Spirit reminded me (because, of course, the enemy started telling me that there was something wrong with me emotionally, that I was feeling that way because of what my husband's touch and hugs or any physical attention represented in the past. It was usually his way of getting whatever he wanted, whether it was to ease his own anxiety, manipulate, or get something he wanted); this is another area where God wants to bring things to the surface so that I can face and address them. I need to be able to separate the past from who I am now in Christ. It's a difficult task to unravel the tangled web of lies and get back to the person that God has designed us to be, but if we allow the Holy Spirit to have His way, He will certainly show us how and do the part that we are unable to on our own. The Holy Spirit can transform us by renewing our minds and how we view people and how we react to situations, but we still must do our part. For the work to be done, we must be partners with Christ in our own healing. Think of it this way: God's going to provide the groceries and all ingredients to make the meal, but He's not going to cook it and spoon-feed us.

Looking back on all of the trials that I've gone through from the beginning of 2020 to now, God has never left me. The Holy Spirit has guided, corrected, ordered my steps, and comforted me through it all the more that I leaned into God and His Word. That is what we should do no matter how the tumultuous waters around us may churn; the key is always staying in the presence of God. One of my favorite psalms sums it all up perfectly "He who dwells in the secret place of the Most High, shall abide under the shelter of the Almighty" (Psalm 91:1–2). The writer speaks about the contentment that comes from resting in God's protection, that when we trust in God, we can feel safe.

October 9, 2021

This morning we woke up, and my husband was checking the return on the air-conditioning unit to see how much water from the condensation had dripped in. Sure enough, it needed to be emptied, and he needed to flush the line. I asked him if he needed me to help, and in the snarky fashion he's used in the past, he said something like, "that would be nice" or "if you want to." That annoyed me, and I know God is definitely working on him because he is not the same man, but still, some behaviors linger, so it annoyed me that he couldn't just say yes or no. So, I said, "Do you need me to help you or not?" He said yes, and I helped. Then a few minutes later, he was aggravatingly looking for something, and I asked, "What are you looking for?" He said he was looking for the short orange Shop-Vac. I stood in the doorway of the garage, staring right at the vacuum cleaner, perplexed as I thought it was the very one he had been looking for. As usual, he had stacked stuff on top of it. I asked him if it was the one he had been looking for, but he said, "No, I'm talking about the one that's orange and medium height, not that one," so I said, "Oh, okay," and tried to suggest places where it could have been. He looked out in the shed and came back in, perplexed, saying he couldn't imagine where it would be. He then turned around and said, "Oh, there it is," and starts moving things off of the very vacuum that I had pointed to earlier. I was so very annoyed because it was common for him to dismiss me or not listen to me. But I know this is something that God wanted to work out of me because what mattered more? Was being right and getting the credit that important? Our flesh wants us to fight and argue, as does the enemy, but what is far more important is building character in us that reflects the image of Jesus Christ. So in this, I turn the other cheek and refrain from the usual snarky comment or argument meant to make him feel foolish. Another lesson learned.

October 11, 2021

What an awful morning! I went to bed early because I was so tired and hadn't gotten enough rest. The enemy really comes in like a thief under the cloak of darkness and attacks all the sensitive and weakest areas of our lives. Everything got on my nerves, work was overly stressful, and I was so overwhelmed that I could barely think, and even my skin felt uncomfortable. This is what the cowardly enemy does: he comes in at a more suitable time when our focus is elsewhere and we are getting pressure from all around, sneaking in the back door and wreaking havoc.

The beauty of belonging to the body of Christ, being His, is that God has us in the palm of His hand and will keep us anchored to Christ the rock. Even though I felt temporarily overwhelmed, I felt that God was with me, and the Holy Spirit was keeping me calm and stable. When we stay plugged in, when we keep our trust and faith in God, there's nothing He won't bring us through! The Word of God says that weapons may form but will not prosper (Isaiah 54:17).

October 12, 2021

Good Things to Come

Today my husband went shopping and brought home flowers for me. I found that so wonderful because I love flowers. He said God brought the flowers to his attention while he was at the grocery store, so he obeyed and bought them for me. I love what God is doing in both of us during this time in our lives and how He is working on us together and in different areas of our lives; God is truly a multitasker.

I was listening to the first episode of Joel Osteen's show on TBN about *You Are Stronger Than You Think,* and he mentioned how sometimes God will leave us in an uncomfortable situation and allow it to continue (even though He didn't create the situation) to use it for our own good. It made me see my situation with the company where I am currently working in a different light. There is something in this situation (in all situations) that I am supposed to learn or get something that God wants me to learn. We can save ourselves a great deal of heartache and stress if we remember that God's hand is in everything in our lives, and at times, I need to remind myself when things start to get to me that God is teaching me something. God has a plan and purpose for everything, and though we may not always see the big picture, He's always working behind the scenes.

Earlier this week, I had asked my husband that, if I hadn't said anything to him about marriage back when we were dating, if he would have ever asked me to marry him. He said, "Eventually." His response confirmed to me that he felt pressured into something he didn't want at the time. That I had heaped unwanted responsibilities upon his shoulders, which was why he would constantly say over the years that I forced him to marry me. He hid it behind the notion that he was just joking, but in truth, he was hiding his bitterness, which brought to mind about fifteen years ago when he decided to quit his job without discussing it with me, saying that he was tired of doing the work for everyone else and wanted to do something for himself. That's where his selfishness came to the surface.

His response, "eventually," struck like a gong to that "not good enough," "not worth it," "not the one" part of me that always made me settle for scraps because I felt I wasn't worth anyone's best, so I accepted what little they chose to give me thinking I deserved it. I stored up rejections and allowed them to create a false narrative in my head. God showed me yesterday why it is so important for me to wait on Him and stop diving in and interfering. If I want my marriage to be restored, I have to take my hands off the wheel and my foot off the gas and allow God to have complete control and the Holy Spirit to be my GPS. God knows better than I do exactly what I need and how to fix what was broken.

I love how my husband said God showed him the flowers and told him I would like them and that he should get them for me. I am so glad that God is the one who is in control; it is such a peaceful realization because I no longer need to depend on my own blind understanding. I'm excited about what lies ahead and what God has in store because I know He will do what is best for us all.

October 14, 2021

God told me that I needed to get out of that "not worthy enough," "not deserving enough" mentality. I realize, well, the Holy Spirit made me realize, that I still have a remnant of that notion that somehow, I am unworthy of whatever blessings God has in store for me. The question is why. It seems to stem from not feeling like I deserve anything over and above. A perfect example is when I purchased a designer handbag that I had researched and wanted for quite a long time, I was embarrassed for anyone at work to see it because I didn't want to be judged. I hid it from people who knew me. I can't insult God when He blesses me exceedingly and abundantly because it comes across as ungrateful. This would open the door to the enemy, and I cannot allow that to happen.

God is truly amazing! My husband just asked me (he hadn't all week) if I had said my prayers this morning; I said not yet, and he told me to pray with him. The prayer was "Do Your Best to Glorify Jesus," and the subject was Matthew 25:14–30, the parable of the five talents, and my goodness, this was a word for me! The person reading the prayer was talking about how we should be less concerned about what others are doing and saying or thinking and more concerned with how we're using, developing, growing, and being good stewards of the gifts God has given us. This spoke to me, and I know this message was for me. "Comparison is the thief of joy" (Grace for Purpose, YouTube[8]). Don't worry about what others have been given, and stir up the gifts and talents (treasures) within you (Colossians 3:23–25; Proverbs 16:3); commit the works of your hands and your plans to the Lord so that His name alone is glorified. The verb "commit to" is from a word meaning "to roll." The idea is to roll or commit all your cares to the Lord. Trusting the Lord with our decisions frees us from preoccupation with our problems.[9]

The parable of the five talents illustrates the faithfulness required of God's servants. The master traveling to a far country implies there was more than enough time to test the faithfulness of the servants. The servants were rewarded based on their faithfulness to carry out their master's instructions, not on the size of their responsibility. The wicked servant was unfaithful. If he had truly feared his master, he would have deposited the money with bankers so that the master would have received his investment back with interest. Instead, he did nothing with it.

The Proverb spoke to me because it's about the gifts that God has given each of us and how we choose to steward those gifts. Choosing not to use those gifts to glorify God and to serve in the body of Christ is an insult to God. It spoke to me because the gift that God has given me is to write, and me not being obedient to write each day and do the work He's placed before me is disobedience. I hadn't seen it that way until the Holy Spirit opened my understanding when reading this proverb. God can choose to raise anyone up and call them to a specific purpose; He doesn't have to use us; we need to see it as a privilege and walk in obedience.

October 15, 2021

Yesterday I had a very good therapy session. My therapist said that she was amazed at how far I'd come in just seven weeks. At first, I had no clear idea of what I wanted, needed to do, or which way to go. She said I clearly recognize what I need to do and have been doing it. She said I've pretty much figured things out on my own and have done a fantastic job of implementing steps in my life. I told her that she did help me to recognize things I would never have seen or clearly known (that I married someone who was just like the person who affected me most negatively in my life). She felt as though I didn't really need goals anymore because I'd exceeded them, so our next sessions would focus on tools to help me deal with situations when people, places, or things trigger a memory or cause me to remember my husband's infidelities—an "exit strategy and successful launch," she called it. She feels that I am no longer in crisis and probably won't need any more therapy unless something comes up that I have difficulty handling. She praised me and gave me kudos, me working in partnership with God! God made me be open even though I did not want to do therapy and went kicking and screaming all the way. I find it difficult and uncomfortable to talk about feelings, and yet, each session brought new discoveries, insights, and steps forward. As she said, she was more of a sounding board with no emotional attachments and helped me talk things out more than anything.

God's hand has been in this with me from the very beginning. The Holy Spirit never let me hide from my issues but brought them to the light and helped me to face them and go through each one so that I could heal and be made whole. He didn't allow me to be lazy with this process or to put off counseling; but held up a mirror to get to the core of why, where, when, and how I found myself at this point in my life. I am so thankful that the Holy Spirit helped me to stay the course! In Exodus 14:13, Moses says to the Israelites, "Do not be afraid. Stand firm and you will see the deliverance the Lord will bring you today. The Egyptians you see today you will never see again." As children of God, we are reminded that we should not fear, no matter what the world around us looks like, no matter what storms come; we must stand firm and rest in His promises, remain in the shelter of His love and trust in His Word "because greater is He that is in you than he that is in the world" (1 John 4:4). There is salvation through the pain; there is healing at the end of the journey if we stay the course.

October 18, 2021

No More Trials?

We, as Christians, can sometimes believe the misconception that once we're saved, everything should be perfect and conflict should just go away or be nonexistent, but that is not based on scripture. Jesus said in John 16:33, "These things I have spoken to you that in Me you may have peace. In this world you will have tribulation [trouble]; but be of good cheer, I have over-come the world," clearly warning us that we will go through tri-als and moments of testing because though we are set apart and are His, we still live in a fallen and sinful world. We will feel moments of pressure and distress, but when we place our trust and faith in Jesus, in the Almighty God, He can give us peace that cannot be explained so that we can persevere and with-stand any pressure the world tries to heap upon our shoulders. We need to remember that no matter what we're faced with, we must never forget that Jesus didn't promise us that things would be perfect but that He will be with us and give us the strength to go through whatever we may face. Yes, it can sometimes be painful, but the freedom, joy, and peace that come after are priceless.

A few months ago, my husband went on a rant about how the more he walks with God and reads the word, the more miserable his life has been. I nearly fell over laughing because, for me, my life has been far more amazing! When I say amazing, I mean that the weight of worry no longer burdens my shoulders. Stress no longer has a choke hold on my life. When I look in the mirror, I see my gray hairs differently! Rather than representing aging, it now represents wisdom to me—how amazing is that? This certain peace comes from resting in God's hands, knowing that He controls all––God, not world leaders or those with money and power, controls the things of this world. His Word says the heart of the king is in His hands to turn any way He chooses. Knowing that God has me in the palm of His hands is such a comfort and allows me to let go of all my cares so that I can relax and not stress over things that don't matter or ones I cannot control.

October 19, 2021

Triggers

My husband and I decided to do date night early in the week and went to see the new James Bond movie. There was a scene in the movie that made me almost take a tumble back into the time when my husband made his confession to me, but I was able to remind myself that it was behind me and that we were moving on from it. I now see what my therapist meant when she spoke about "triggers." Seeing the scene in James Bond triggered a memory of one of the instances where my husband was unfaithful, and all of those images came flooding in. I sat there in the theater, wondering if he was doing any reminiscing of his own. I found myself in a very uncomfortable spot where his infidelity was playing in my head like a movie, and I wondered if this was how it went for him. I found myself no longer enjoying the date time, and resentment crept in. Instead of enjoying the movie, I recounted the many betrayals. Hearing his voice at that moment even irritated me because of what he had done, not just to me but to our relationship. These are the things God wants me to face and work on because there will be instances, even years from now, that may trigger a memory and take me back to what happened, that I need to master it and not let it master me and toss me around like a rag doll. My counselor asked me, "What do you do when those triggers happen?" At first, I struggled with that because everything was so new and fresh, but my answer to her weeks later was to take back control! In order to take control, I needed to go to counseling to get to what was at the core of my insecurities and false beliefs about myself so that I could sever those far-reaching tentacles.

God is so amazing in how He handles His children. There is nothing He won't use to teach, grow, and heal us. I was getting dressed for work this morning, which is more of a ritual than anything else because I get dressed to go to the living room to sit at my makeshift "workspace." It was 8:50 a.m., and I was stressed over what underwear to put on with a powder blue lace bra that I had picked out. I kept looking and got frustrated because I could not find an exact match for the bra. I asked aloud, "Why do I care so much about whether my underwear (that no one ever sees) matches my bra?" The Holy Spirit took me back to my prom in 1987 when I was walking into the hotel where our prom was being held over Paradise Island in the Bahamas (where I grew up). I was walking up the walkway that led to the roped-off carpet where spectators had crowded around (many of them grown women), criticizing and marveling at the attire. For whatever reason, our school's proms were the event of the season, like some sort of fashion show people would watch and comment on the fashion.

A little back story on my dress: I purchased the fabric that my aunt made my dress from. It was a shiny royal blue, and I had to have shoes dyed to match my dress. I took a swatch of fabric to a local shoe store to have shoes dyed to match my dress. My shoes were ready before my aunt finished my dress, so I got the dress the night of the prom and was disappointed when I saw them up against the dress because the color was a shade off. It was too late to do anything about it, and I had no other options, so I wore the shoes and hoped that no one would notice. So, I walked the carpet into the venue with my date and heard a grown woman say out loud, "Her shoes don't even match her dress," and that must have hurt something deep inside because here I am almost forty years later fussing over whether the underwear that will be hidden under my clothes matches my bra!

It is so amazing how a relationship with God can transform our lives in such an amazing way that there is no fear in looking at yourself in the mirror and admitting what issues you have and facing them. The blinders come off, and you're wide open to His truth, the *only* truth that brings healing. We are His and made in His image. How can you be healed from something that you won't admit, acknowledge, or recognize? Yes, it can sometimes be painful to face those tough truths about ourselves, but just like an infected wound needs to be debrided (which means to remove damaged tissue or foreign objects from a wound) so that healthy tissue can grow, we need to bring those things to the surface so God can remove the infecting lies of the enemy. God wants to remove the damaged, hurting parts of us so that healing can take place, and as the Bible says, "Whom the Son sets free is free indeed" (John 8:36).

October 20, 2021

Intimacy

A word oftentimes incorrectly associated with sexual kind of relations or closeness, but it means so much more. We have no real understanding of what real, true intimacy is or that closeness can only come when we experience and understand God's unfailing love.

"Intimacy" is defined as a "close familiarity or friendship; closeness."[10] A close relationship where we don't have to put on airs, don't have to hide our shortcomings because the other person knows the deepest parts of us, faults and all, and loves us with such an amazing love—only God can provide that type of relationship. To become more intimate with a person, we must get to know them, study their character, know their likes or dislikes, and understand them. A person opens up more and welcomes you into their inner circle when you show them that you care and are trustworthy. In the same way, God wants us to get to know Him by knowing His character through His word, prayer, and worship. In Hebrew, the word *yadah* is used to describe intimacy or closeness. The word means "to throw" or "the extended hand, to throw out the hand" and is used to describe worship. Worship is intimacy with God and something that we often take for granted, and we forget how necessary it is for us to draw closer to God.

God already knows us better than we know ourselves: we are the ones who must get to know Him, and the only way to do that is through reading the Bible and seeing how His character is displayed throughout the Bible, the greatest love story ever told. Having a one-on-one personal relationship with God is a growing friendship and partnership that grows deeper over time. If we would only apply this to our human relationships or relations (where we take the time to learn one another's love languages, likes, and dislikes or have mutual respect for one another), they would be more fruitful and satisfying.

October 21, 2021

It has been a rough week (I know I say this a lot, but things have certainly been ramping up in my life over the past two years, and it comes in waves), and not in the way one would think but more because I feel the weight of something. Something trying to latch on and bring me down and drag me under. A wrong word uttered, an ask at work that seemed over the top or the last straw, a malaise that smacks of a spiritual battle. A struggle or muddled mind to pray. Disinterest in reading the Word...a spiritual attack!

The enemy knows how and when to attack us, a lack of sleep, a distracting crisis in the family, etc. Psalm 105 tells us to rejoice and worship the Lord and search for the Lord and His strength. I think when I am tired, the doubt tries to take hold, and I say, "tries," because no matter what it looks like, I believe God for *every* word He's spoken, every promise and covenant made; I know it will come to pass. And I'm not just talking about the worldly things He has promised, but the restoration and salvation. I trust God because there is nothing in the world that can even come close to giving me the hope, peace, and love that

God has given us through Jesus Christ! I'm getting excited just writing about it.

Psalm 105 also mentions how God tested Joseph's character before He brought the promise to pass. We need to be reminded of God's faithfulness even when we're being faithless or struggling in our walk; God keeps His word and never breaks a promise made. He puts us in situations where our character is tested to make sure that we can handle the promise because He will never give us anything that would destroy us.

When we are saved, Satan must ask permission from God to do anything to us. In Luke 22:31, Jesus tells Peter that Satan has asked for him. Jesus says Satan wanted to sift the disciple as wheat, meaning he must get permission to try to destroy our faith in God so forcefully to get believers to turn away from God, just as he tried to do with Job. Jesus prayed for Peter that he would be strengthened in his faith and would not fall. Isn't it great to be a child of the Most High God? That we have our Lord and Savior, Jesus Christ, praying for us to be strengthened in our faith? The single most important thing that the adversary wants to attack isn't your finances, home, car, or job; he wants to destroy our faith (John 10:10). So, during times of attack, we need to lean into God's Word and remind ourselves of the promises, see the struggles other believers like Peter went through and how they persevered; this is how we build and strengthen our faith. Though what Jesus prophesied to Peter came to pass, and he did deny Christ, Peter got up and dusted himself off and went on to strengthen his other brethren. We must remember that when we go through trials, they are to refine our character and strengthen our faith (James 1:2–4, 12; 1 Peter 1:6–7) and to make us more the image of Christ (Romans 8:29). We not only experience these troubles to reinforce our own faith but also to share our experiences with others so that they too can be lifted up, strengthened in their faith, and can overcome. This is why it is so important for us to share our testimonies with others and to be obedient to whatever call God has on our lives; because we are being equipped to help lead others to salvation.

It is so comforting to know that when we are experiencing challenges in our Christian walk, Jesus is in the midst of the storm with us to give us His strength and as the greatest intercessor (Philippians 4:13, Romans 8:26–39, Hebrews 7:25) on our behalf and that Satan's ability to sift us like wheat is restricted by the intercession of Christ.

October 22, 2021

I thank God for bringing me to the end of a very rough week. I feel physically and mentally drained. Thank God for His grace and tender mercies that He never leaves nor forsakes us. That even when we are struggling in the darkness, He steps into the void and reaches for us to pull us out. He woke me up this morning at 7:30 a.m. and said, "Walk." Now while I realize that He was getting me back into the routine that kept me grounded in Him:

1. pray
2. exercise (which for me means walking)
3. worship
4. read the Word
5. write

But now, as I write this, I realize "walk" means "walk with Me." How absolutely amazing is that? Walk with Him and get in His presence—this is what sustains me and allows me to endure. God is so very gracious, and it's like medicine for my soul. Nothing else matters except being close to Him and walking with Him. The Bible says to "seek first the kingdom…" (Matthew 6:33). Seeking Jesus and His righteousness and God's sovereign rule, getting to know our Lord and Savior and the character of God, and everything else that we need will be given to us, meaning God will take care of the rest.

Today I realized that my husband struggles greatly with his old selfishness and almost seems to hang onto his old self. I say almost because I know in my heart that God will change him because that is my prayer for him.

October 26, 2021

Believing in Rebirth

It is sometimes hard to let go of old hurts and past failures and remember that old things have passed away, but we have to trust that God's divine plans for us are perfect if we submit our will to Him. We also need to remember that we died and were resurrected with Jesus.

October 27, 2021

Last night I struggled to get comfortable in bed and had a difficult time falling asleep. The realization in my mind that I've failed in some part of my life, the most important part—this is why it's so important for us to give all of our cares to God. But more importantly, what I have learned is that sometimes God will not allow us to rest easy because He is calling us into His presence because He knows we are carrying a burden that only He can shoulder and wants to relieve us of the weight. At first, I would toss and turn when I was restless in bed, fall asleep hours later and wake up exhausted and sometimes with a headache. When I finally heard the Holy Spirit urging me to get up and worship or get up and pray or to get up and simply sit in God's presence, only then was I able to find peaceful sleep. Worship requires us to give something of ourselves by bowing to God's sovereignty and allowing the Spirit to lead us, not worship however and whenever we feel like it. There is a relationship, fellowship, and revelation when we enter into the presence of God through worship. Think of it as bringing gifts to the altar in a way that is pleasing to God and Him showering you with love because of your heartfelt sacrifice. This is such an important part of our Christian walk and our growth. I admit that it took me a long time to grasp the idea of worship, and I thought that I needed to be on my face, filled with the Holy Spirit and speaking in tongues to truly worship; but the truth is that just as our Christian walk is individual (no two are alike), how God wants us to worship is also personal and individual. Some may hear the voice of God while listening to a specific song that only they and God share. Or for another, sitting quietly after listening to worship music may be the way God ushers them into His presence; and for others, it can be a combination which is why we need to allow God to tell us how He wants to be worshipped.

October 28, 2021

I had my seventh therapy session today, and we talked again about triggers and things that caused me to go back to the painful place involving my husband's infidelity. As I sit here, I am sad because I am not sure where we go from here. I look at my husband, and I'm sad because of the conversation we had recently about the fact that I thought that we should possibly divorce and go our separate ways to save me the pain and so that he can get what he needs since he felt at some point that I wasn't giving him what he needed so that he could find someone who can. Almost as if he didn't do anything wrong and the ownness was on me. I know that I have forgiven him, but the forgetting part is the challenge. The part I am struggling with is that I am acting as if I must make this work or fix this. It's God who is doing the work; I need to follow His plan. I need to remind myself that I need to let the Holy Spirit guide me as to what to do and do it; God will take care of the rest. As I write this, God gives me Isaiah 54:17,

"No weapon formed against you shall prosper, And every tongue which rises against you in judgment,

You shall condemn. This is the heritage of the servants of the Lord, And their righteousness is from Me," says the LORD.

So no matter what devices or schemes the enemy may craft against us as children of God, they will all fail, and God has given us the words and the power to dispute them when we walk in faith; their devious works will fail, and whatever instrument of war they fashion against us will not succeed.

Friend, remember the enemy will certainly attack us in areas where we seem most vulnerable and feed us lies about who we are, but we must speak God's Word to the enemy and declare that any weapon formed will not prosper because our protection comes from the Lord.

October 29, 2021

Today was a day chock-full of challenges. I was extremely overwhelmed at work; my husband had struggles with his boss, and the boss's second-in-command spoke to him with such disrespect that I was angry. A coworker who was assigned to me because she had failed in the position she was in and was demoted had been given a last chance to work with me in helping me as a processor but quit after only working in her new position for less than two months, so more responsibility was piled on me yet again. Then I was contacted by a former work colleague whom I hadn't heard from in a few years, wanting to talk to me about a job opportunity. I eagerly let this person call me to pitch a consultancy-type job with no benefits because of the overwhelming drowning feeling I was going through at my current job. I ignored the fact that this was not a trustworthy person and that the people my former coworker wanted around and carried to each new job opportunity were equally untrustworthy. This was a more "opportune time" for the enemy because I was able to ignore what God had shown me about this person early on in my working at the same company; I was also told about the character of this person by former coworkers who had been burned and betrayed by this person, yet I let my flesh lead me through a door that God did not open. I sought wise counsel from another sister in Christ who told me that she did not have a good feeling about the opportunity, yet months later when the company reached out to me and offered me a position paying me three times what I am currently being paid, I jumped at the opportunity despite the nagging in my spirit and the dread that came over me. Here I was, taking on something that I knew I should not and letting the high pay rate and the thought of extra money be my guide.

The enemy studies us—that's Scripture—and his tactics are crafty and deceptive, and he tries to fool the saints by trying to mimic God but cannot. I talked myself into taking the job, saying that the extra money would be good, it would allow me to pay off bills and afford me the opportunity to leave my current job, but the Holy Spirit would have us ignorant of nothing, and God used my friend to remind me that I would be walking into a pit of vipers. That still, small voice kept telling me that if I were to take on this second job, it would cut deeply into my time spent with God, my writing time, and family time as well, but it took me a few weeks to actually listen and finally send an email thanking them for their offer, but that I could not move forward. Friends, remember not every open door is of God; sometimes it's a test, sometimes it's a trap; we must listen to what the Holy Spirit is telling us, not what feels good to our flesh or sounds good to our logical minds. Jesus said in John 10:27–28, "My sheep hear My voice, and I know them, and they follow Me. And I give them eternal life, and they shall never perish; neither shall anyone snatch them out of My hand." We must listen to that still, small voice, that gut feeling, and ask ourselves why we are doing what we are doing.

Seeking wise counsel from other believers further along in their walk is a very important part of our walk as well. We are supposed to bear each other's burdens and lift each other up and share the load; that is what my friend did for me. She reminded me why I did not like working with this person and why I was happy getting away from the toxic environment and also reminded me that not all opportunities are from God. Throughout the day, I felt as though I needed a break from all of the pressure. I read some Scripture and listened to a few worship songs, but I felt like I was drowning under the crashing waves. We must ask ourselves: How do we properly equip ourselves for the full-on attacks of the enemy? Because all he needs is to see a small crack in the armor, and he'll exploit it until the dam breaks and the waters come gushing forth. I had to remind myself that I needed to reach for the life preserver (Jesus) before the storm came. Jesus says that He is the way, the truth, and the life! He is the One who is with us in the fire, so it doesn't scorch us, the one who is with us in times of trouble and great testing. The only One who has the power to save. Just like a receding wave exposes seaweed or trash left behind on a beach, the attacks of the enemy do the same thing. It exposes areas where we are weak and places we need to shore up and strengthen.

This is a journey where I go from glory to glory, a partnership with God holding everything in His hands and Jesus leading the way. I am not the same person I used to be; I am growing every day, learning from the Master, and always getting better as I humble myself, self-reflect, and allow the Holy Spirit to be my guide. Like Peter, we may fall along the way, but what matters is that we get up and continue on the path that God has set us on, strengthening one another in the body of Christ.

October 31, 2021

I was reading Psalm 104 today, and the Holy Spirit just gave me something I'm so amazed at. There's so much Scripture that we read that points to God's infinite wisdom, His mercy, and His grace and how it went into creation that our minds can't even fathom. We hear the saying beauty for ashes so often, but we don't think about how fire consumes and utterly destroys whatever it touches, yet when the flames cease and the ground cools, new life springs forth, new greenery shooting up from the rich and fertile soil created from the ashes, and we see new life pushing through. So, when you think about it, think about how, from the storms of life, whether they be by a fire that consumes and licks through a family, seemingly destroying everything, wonder how it can then bring forth life. From destruction and ruin? Old things restored and made new is something amazing, truly amazing! We don't even know the depths of how intricate God's plans are; we could live a lifetime and never know nor understand the ways of God. He says His ways are not our ways and His thoughts are not our thoughts; they are far beyond. We would see that every day if we stop and just read His Word and take in what's around us; we would see the beauty that God has for His children and what He's put in us...just amazing.

November 1, 2021

God is the scaffolding that we stand upon to reach heights we couldn't get to on our own. He takes us places and takes us to heights we could not achieve on our own merit or skill.

This world will pitch self-help and will push you to be aggressive to achieve your goals, but without Him, we can do nothing. Jesus said in John 15:5–6,

> I am the vine, you are the branches. He who abides in Me, and I in him, bears much fruit; for without Me you can do nothing. If anyone does not abide in Me, he is cast out as a branch and is withered; and they gather them and throw them into the fire, and they are burned.

God's Word is clear: we can do nothing without Jesus, without submitting to His will and allowing Him to guide us. The path to healing, peace, and purpose is through the Vine that feeds, supports, and sustains us. We should not be fooled by what the world counts as success, happiness, or contentment because these things are mere distractions and not based on truth. Scripture says the prince of this world is Satan and his ultimate goal is to lure man into his snare of pride and lust of the flesh by encouraging us to chase after fleshly desires that are meant to corrupt the souls of the human race. When we put our trust in material things or the things this world has to offer, we give control of our lives over to the enemy so that when he rips the rug out from under us, and we lose everything, or things don't work out as planned, we are thrown into the pit of despair which gives the enemy a foothold and draws us away from God. He fools us into thinking that we can do things of our own power and make things happen on our own, but what Jesus speaks about is spiritual fruit, lasting fruit. The branches that are cast out are those who are not saved, those who choose to live life without ever having known Christ.

Fruit cannot grow to maturity without being connected to the branches; the branch cannot sustain and bear fruit unless it is connected to and drawing its sustaining life source from the vine itself—a lifeline. The world will offer much that draws us down the broad path, but it cannot sustain us, and from it springs no spiritual fruit but rather thorns and thistles. No one knows what we need as God does. We spend so much time seeking out the opinions of others, so much time searching the internet for guidance, comparing our lives to others, and taking a path we are not meant to travel. Why not seek the One who wrote the manual for your life? God said, "Before you were born, I sanctified you" (Jeremiah 1:5). Do you know how powerful that is? God whose breath spoke this world into existence, God whose hand controls the universe, knows everything about you. Despite what you've done, despite what happened to you, what people have said or done to you, He has approved you, and He has great plans for you (Jeremiah 29:11). If only you seek Him through His living Word (through Christ, the only way to the Father), everything you need will be given to you (Matthew 6:33), not wait until things are better in your life or that you are no longer broken. We need to seek God before we do anything else; that means repenting and confessing our sins, asking God's forgiveness, recognizing Jesus as your Lord and Savior, and everything we need (whether healing from addiction, being set free from bondage, being released from the shame or guilt of something we have done) will be given freely to us.

God is faithful; what He says in His word, He will do. Just as He parted the Red Sea for the Israelites when He brought them out of Egypt, He will clear a path to wholeness, a path that leads you to righteousness that only He can provide. He will also release the waters of the Red Sea once you've passed through (just like He did when the Israelites were on dry ground and the pharaoh's army tried to pursue them) to wash away and drown the enemy and the lies he whispers, drown out and wash away what the enemy once used to hold you in bondage. God may not bring all of the storms into our lives, but He certainly controls them so they don't threaten to consume us and lay waste to our lives. He will bring out of the storm those of us who diligently seek Him and will use the experience to strengthen and refine us and to help someone else. We cannot let the world feed us lies, telling us that we are victims because of what has happened to us; we are more than conquerors through Christ who strengthens us. Jesus questioned the man at the pool of Bethesda, who was crippled and had been coming to this pool for thirty-eight years, hoping for healing. When Jesus saw him,

He asked him, "Do you want to be made well?" He didn't ask how the man got that way or why he was there, or what happened to him. He asked if he wanted to be made whole, set free from the disability that crippled him for most of his life, meaning that we have a choice: healing is yours if you seek it. Jesus didn't care about his excuses; Jesus didn't ask the man for an elaborate demonstration of faith and that then he would be healed; He simply told the man to rise and walk. If you believe that Christ can heal you, you are healed, whether it's through the right medical treatment, a counselor, or a miracle of you picking up your sickbed, so to speak, and walking. However, God chooses to heal you in whatever way He chooses, you need only surrender to His will and power, and He will set you free. Sometimes the healing may not look the way we want it to, or perhaps a loved one may succumb to an illness, but that does not mean God is not faithful. Remember: His ways are not our ways and we must trust Him.

Without Jesus, without a relationship with God, we can do nothing. God's Word is a lamp unto our feet and a light to our path. When you look at the word "scaffolding," it is a temporary structure on the outside of a building, made usually of wooden planks and metal poles, used by workers while building, repairing, or cleaning the building. According to the KJV dictionary, "scaffold" means a structure among builders, an assemblage or structure of timbers, boards, or planks, erected by the wall of a building to support the workmen.[11]

"Scaffolding": (1) a structure for support in an elevated place, (2) that which sustains; a frame; as the scaffolding of the body, (3) temporary structure for support (*Webster's American Diction-*

ary of the English Language). God isn't asking us to be perfect, self-sufficient, all cleaned up, polished, and shiny. He wants you to come to Him with all the broken pieces, all the hidden, messy places of your life—bring it all to Him and lay your burdens down on the altar before the throne of grace (Matthew 11:28); all that crushing guilt and heavy pain, lay it down, surrender it all to God and allow the blood of Jesus to cover it and wash it away. God is the one who scrubs us clean and cleanses us from sin (Psalm 51:7). He is the One who makes us new. Jesus gives us a chance at rebirth, where we become new creatures, and all that is old (our past, our mistakes, what was done to us, what was said about us) passes away and is no more.

God provides the support system for us as we grow and strengthen in our walk with Christ; the scaffolding that He provides are His Word, other believers in the body of Christ, and the Holy Spirit. We just need to come to the throne and be willing to let go and submit completely to God.

November 2, 2021

What an eventful day we had yesterday! I sat here writing and spending time with God and letting the Holy Spirit flow through me, and we had a good rhythm going. Then my husband came over and sat next to me to tell me what I thought was a dream, but it was actually him telling me how he didn't feel well and that he had a rough night. I admit I was quite annoyed because he was interrupting my groove. He asked me if he should call his doctor to see if he could get in. I said he should and went back to writing. He then brought his phone back (he was on hold), so I stayed with his phone until he came out of the shower. I spoke to the service because the office was bombarded by calls, so we were told to call back. I gave him back the phone, annoyed because he had interrupted my time with God.

He came back out and said he needed to go to urgent care but was feeling dizzy. I asked him if he needed me to drive him. Again annoyed—he vacillated, and I said I'd have to call my boss to let her know. Then he apologized; it was then that I realized I was behaving poorly, and the Holy Spirit convicted me. This was a time of crisis, and my husband needed me; God wanted me to behave with love and kindness, and I did not. I was more worried about my own needs and feelings.

I took a shower and drove him to urgent care, and he was sent to the ER because they believed it was diverticulitis and he may have a ruptured colon. He was in quite a bit of pain and began to cry when he told me that he needed a CT scan. I comforted him, telling him that he was in the hands of the chief physician, the ultimate healer, and he needed to pray and believe for healing. I want to stop here for a beat and say that when you're born again and have a personal relationship with God, something miraculous happens. The burden of unforgiveness is no longer your cross to bear; releasing that burden of unforgiveness to Jesus allows His blood and grace to cover the hurt and allows you to find compassion and peace again. I'm not minimizing what happened to you or what someone may have done to you; what I am saying is that when you allow God in, He can take that thing that once crippled you, held you hostage, or may have ruined you; into a thing of no effect, a thing that draws you into a closer walk with Him where that thing that nearly destroyed you is no longer a weapon the enemy can use against you.

I walked into the ER with my husband, not a victim of his cheating and years of damage from his brokenness, but as a victor, an overcomer, and a wife. I prayed for him: I asked God to spare him and, whatever it might be, to heal him. I held his hand, encouraged him, and attended to his needs. He looked over at me and said I was a good wife. I then realized that God wanted me to do this. Sitting there supporting him, being his wife, was a breakthrough moment. Weeks before, the "what next" question depressed me because I had no idea where my husband and I would go next. When we let God into our situations and allow the Holy Spirit in and allow Him to have His way, it allows us to let go of grudges, slights, pain, etc., and allows God to work on us. If we follow the lead of the Holy Spirit, that's when we realize that the pain is less and less until it no longer controls us. When we surrender to God, He takes care of all the details.

I felt so full of peace, sitting there supporting my husband, praying for and encouraging him. So many thoughts ran through my mind. We prayed, and God answered our prayers: not only did the CT show no need for surgery, but there was no perforation, and the infection was minor and could be treated with antibiotics. When we trust God, when we have faith in Him, He will move mountains on our behalf; we have to trust in Him (Psalm 37:4–5).

November 3, 2021

Have you ever heard the sound of rain, but there is no rain? I was sitting here on the couch, asking God to speak to me, and was listening. I heard outside the sound of pouring rain, and the Holy Spirit reminded me of Elijah when he heard the sound of rain. In 1 Kings 18:41–46, Elijah heard the sound of rain before it came. The wonderful sound of the blessings and promises to come!

Life in the desert is when we are refined and faith is tested. Character is tested during times of drought. What does our character say about us when things are difficult and nothing seems to be working? Do you look for someone to blame, or do you draw closer to God and let your faith deepen? These are showers of blessing that come after a long drought, and through it all, Elijah remained faithful to God. When in the desert, we must remember God's promises to us because the abundance of rain is on the way. Showers of blessings. The drought is as good as over. We should not give up on people who seem far away from God; we should pray for them and bless them (verse 41). They are not our enemies; we need to pray for them and bless them—do our part and leave the rest to God.

Our hearts should be changed when God reveals Himself to us and performs miracles in our lives (1 Kings 18:39), as He did on Monday with my husband and the diverticulitis. As we go from glory to glory, there should be a marked change in us that is obvious to those around us. When you let God's voice be louder than the voice of the enemy, there is healing, freedom, and wholeness that come along with listening to God's voice and letting His word be the authority in your life. You are not a victim of your circumstances or a product of your environment, as some would say; God's Word says that we are more than conquerors through Christ who strengthens us (Romans 8:37). It is God who brings the victory (Exodus 14:14, Jeremiah 1:19).

We have a real enemy, and his name is Satan. Scripture calls him our adversary; in Hebrew, it's the word tsar, which comes from the word tsarar and, according to Strong, means "narrow, a tight place (usually figuratively, i.e., trouble); also a pebble, an opponent; adversary, afflicted(-tion), anguish, close, distress, enemy, flint, foe, narrow, small, strait, tribulation, trouble."[12] He is a pebble in our shoe, the enemy lurking in the darkness, just waiting to steal our joy, rob us of a full life, and threaten our faith in God, which to him is the ultimate goal—to turn us away from God and the path that Jesus cleared for us. Paul encourages us to stand firm against these many attacks mentioned in Romans 8:35–39 because Jesus has guaranteed the victory and gives us the power to defeat the enemy. Nothing that we go through is a surprise to God because Scripture tells us that the devil came down to the earth, full of hatred for mankind because he knows that his time here is short (Revelation 12:12), but Satan has no power and is incapable of snatching us from God's hand or separating us from the love of God. Through our faith in Jesus Christ as our Lord and Savior, we are His and are under His protection; isn't that an awesome place to be? That when we go through testing and trouble, we can say, "I can do this," no matter how forceful the storm, no matter how it may bring us to our knees and make us feel as though we can't go any further; Jesus is in the midst of the storm with us, and we can rest in the knowledge that at the finish line God is waiting with open arms. While Jesus clearly tells us in scripture that we will have trials and go through tribulations, God promises to deliver us from them all. We must remember what Jesus tells us in John 10:27–29,

> My sheep listen to my voice; I know them, and they follow me. I give them eternal life, and they shall never perish; no one will snatch them out of my hand. My Father, who has given them to me, is greater than all; no one can snatch them out of my Father's hand.

November 5, 2021

Struggles and Failures

Have you ever been in a place where you feel yourself being dragged back to old habits and powerless to stop it? Or as if people have expectations of you that hold you to a standard that seems unattainable or unfair?

We need to surrender to God every day and let the Holy Spirit do His work in us because each time we try to handle anything, whether emotional, physical, mental, or spiritual, we must first give control over to the One who controls all and sees all; otherwise, we fail or cause undue harm to ourselves. This is what failing at doing things without seeking God, calling on the Holy Spirit, or including Him in everything we do looks like, "Today, everything that my family did irritated me and made me feel annoyed." I felt they were selfish, rude, inconsiderate, and petty. It's so easy to see other people's faults and shortcomings and ignore your own because it takes the focus off of you and allows you to push down the pain or emotion and pretend for just a moment that your issue doesn't exist and you're fine when you're not. This behavior is what drags you back to the past, dredging up old feelings, past hurts, and old slights and using them as some sort of false salve to those wounds that we won't allow God to expose and touch. It's a false sense of peace that when we give in to it, it's like a setback to healing. That's what the enemy wants; remember: he studies each and every one of us and knows how to keep us in bondage. Anytime we feel pain, the first instinct is to avoid the source of the pain rather than to allow God to help us to face our issues. We allow the enemy to keep us broken and damaged when we ignore the freedom that Jesus offers when we lay the burdens we carry at the foot of the cross.

What does that look like when you feel all the pain of whatever you're going through? Looking to God every step of the way is what breaks the cycle and breaks yokes and strongholds. God hears us when we call on Him; He rescues us from all of our troubles (Psalm 50:15). All He asks is that we trust in Him and are obedient to His Word. Be submissive to Jesus's teachings and let the voice of God be louder than the voice of the enemy; let God be truth and every man, every person, thing, and enemy—a lie!

November 7, 2021

God's grace is truly sufficient. When we accept His grace (God's unmerited favor, special privilege toward His unworthy children), He is willing to forgive and bless His wayward children despite our shortcomings and the fact that we are undeserving (Romans 3:23, Romans 5:1–2). *Merriam-Webster* defines grace as "unmerited divine assistance given humans for their regeneration or sanctification, approval or favor."[13]

I am grateful to be called His and even more grateful to be living under grace because it is the only way that I can survive the day-to-day challenges and not resort to old behaviors. Under grace is a beautiful place to be because the burdens we carry, whether due to our own actions or the actions of others, are no longer ours to bear. This weekend my husband made me reevaluate our situation, and I started to wonder what I'm going to get out of a situation I did not create and from someone who has done so much to hurt me but yet has expectations of me. The Holy Spirit reminded me that it is God who is doing the work in both of us, and we both need to be obedient to the path He has us on. My walk, healing, and growth are not going to look like anyone else's, and I have to remember that! I can't keep reaching into the past for the hammer of memory to bludgeon my husband with it if I want to heal, grow, and become a mature believer. You have to remember that you're not the only person ever to hurt or be hurt. God knows our every wound and loves each one of His children and knows how to provide everything we need even when we don't know ourselves, even if it's a good swift kick in the behind. I've had many instances of tough correction during this journey, and while it was painful, it was for my good. God had to remind me that just because he did so much to hurt me, that didn't give me the right to mistreat him; God is the one who justifies and makes things right. He will not fight for us when we're busy fighting against Him. Think of it this way: God is not going to step into the ring to fight our battles when we're standing in the ring fighting on our own. The Holy Spirit reminded me that it's not the snide remark from my husband that matters (of course, God cares how others treat us, but He deals with His children and doesn't need our help to do so) but rather why it hurt my feeling so deeply and makes me so mad. We spend so much time focusing on small things that are insignificant that we miss the big thing that has a significant impact on our lives.

For years, I've never liked being joked with and always thought it was rude to make fun of someone or to embarrass someone, so I would always get upset when my husband or children did it to me. I would get upset and find it cruel and what was really happening deep down inside was a great sense of hurt that I was too afraid to acknowledge or recognize because it exposed my low self-esteem, low self-worth, and feeling of never being good enough. I was also notorious for making snide comments about others, which was ironic because it's the very thing I didn't like having done to me.

In 2016, when my father passed away, I felt as if I was set adrift and so far from the shore that I couldn't find my way back. I couldn't believe it was real. A hole so big grew in my heart that I felt it was exploding out of my chest. A cruel blow, the once vibrant, energetic, brilliant man was no longer with us. I longed to hear his voice and had a hard time processing the reality of it all. He was lying cold in a casket, being shipped in the belly of a plane as freight; the pain was devastating. When I cried, it came from a well so deep inside of me that I never knew it existed. All I wanted to do was reminisce and share all my wonderful memories of the man who loved me so much and demonstrated such great love. I went out to dinner with my family and was telling them a story about when we were children, and my son interrupted, "Mom, you've literally told that story like a million times," then my husband chimed in and said, "Yeah, really," and everyone laughed but me. I went quiet because I was devastated; it hurt me so deeply because I missed Daddy so much, and all I wanted to do was talk about the memories that made me smile and brought me joy. What their behavior said to me was that they didn't have enough love or compassion to accommodate me and listen to my story with hearts filled with love; I was heartbroken. To them, it was a minor petty thing, but it was deeper than that. This is why we must be careful how we handle others (myself included) because we have no idea what inner battles they may be facing and the damage our words may cause despite the fact that they may be smiling on the outside.

Jesus said, "With lovingkindness have I drawn you" (Jeremiah 31:23, KJV)—an everlasting and faithful love. We must learn to have compassion and treat one another with love and kindness, and when we cannot, allow God's grace to cover it. What that means to me is to stay quiet and avoid saying something that would hurt God and grieve the Holy Spirit because we've done or said something to hurt another person.

What I've realized now is back then, I expected everyone else to manage my feelings, which isn't fair. We must learn how to verbalize our needs and to speak up with love when someone does something that we feel is an offense. Jesus teaches us not to hang on to an offense and not hold slights against each other but rather address it and move on from it. When we hold onto offenses, it opens a door that the enemy comes traipsing through, and hurt feelings snowball from there, and soon, you find yourself digging up everything a person ever did to you, and the hurt turns into something else.

So, today, when my husband said something foolish, asked a petty question, or behaved stingily, I practiced restraining myself and calling on the Holy Spirit not only to put a guard around my mouth but also to take captive those negative and spiteful thoughts. As we mature and grow as believers in Christ, we are held to a higher standard and do not act out of our flesh because we are to represent Christ. So, when we encounter negative behaviors, we must act out of love. I'm learning to allow God's love and light to take center stage in my life so that way the enemy's tricks and schemes cannot find room on the stage to steal it.

November 8, 2021

Dry Bones

I woke up this morning and went into worship (Ezekiel 37:1–14). I spoke to God, and I'm sure God saw what has been so heavy in my heart this past week and perhaps longer. I don't know where my marriage is headed and wondered if I was trying to make something work that never really did and was never meant to. I turned on the daily prayer for today on YouTube and the prayer titled "A Blessed Morning. A Prayer for Restoration & Revival | God is About to Do a New Thing in Your Life" (Grace for Purpose, YouTube) and the subject scripture was Ezekiel 37:1–14, the Valley of Dry Bones. I was so amazed at how God speaks to us! And yes, He does indeed speak to us! He was sitting with me, telling me that nothing is too far gone for Him to resurrect and restore it. God is a multitasker, as I've mentioned before, and as He's also working on me with my counseling, He's also working on my husband and, at the same time, our marriage. The Holy Spirit urged me to go deeper in the study of Ezekiel 37, and that led me to a study through which God spoke to me so powerfully that it brought me to my knees in worship and thanksgiving!

God took away my despair and doubt by making me realize that the restoration of our relationship and our marriage started with life that became the valley of dry bones. That I needed to prophesy life over the valley and that life-giving restoration that only God can do first starts with believing that God can do anything and faith in the fact that He will do it. Just like He asked Ezekiel as he stood looking out at a landscape that looked dead and long gone, "Son of man, can these bones live?" (Ezekiel 37:3). He was getting Ezekiel to activate his faith. A good foundation of a relationship begins with trust. We must trust and believe that God can and will do what He promises in His Word. He instructed Ezekiel to put his faith to work: "Prophecy to these dry bones, and say to them, 'O dry bones, hear the word of the LORD!'" (Ezekiel 37:4).

The Holy Spirit made me see that I need to shake off the doubt and believe that nothing is impossible or too difficult for God to accomplish. That I need to believe, activate my faith, and prophecy to my marriage, "Dry bones, hear the word of the Lord!" What brought me to my knees was when the Holy Spirit made me realize that the bones weren't just made flesh, got up whole, and walked. God was clear in Ezekiel's vision; it was a step-by-step process. "I will put sinews on you and bring flesh upon you, cover you with skin and put breath in you, and you shall live. Then you shall know that I am the LORD" (Ezekiel 37:6). So, while it may look like nothing's happening or things have gotten stagnant, God is behind the scenes attaching sinew to the dry bones, preparing the structure for Him to build life onto something long thought dead—we need only believe!

November 10, 2021

I admit that I've allowed myself to be incredibly over-whelmed with the holidays as I watch my credit-card debt go up (which for me is a big no-no), my finances shrink (not enough to cover my bills, but God provides each month, so we are behind on nothing), plans for the holidays are not shaping up to look the way I had envisioned, and I feel let down. The trouble with us wanting things our way or the way we want them to be is that we tend to forget the promises God has made in His Word and what He's promised us personally and allow doubt to creep in. Doubt that He will do what He promised, doubt whether we actually heard from God or made it up, doubt that we are wor-thy of such blessings (which, newsflash, we are not! But we live under the covering of grace). Doubt is the opposite of faith and some synonyms for "doubt," according to the *Oxford American Writer's Thesaurus*, are "skepticism, distrust, mistrust, lack of trust, doubtfulness, suspicion, cynicism, disbelief, incredulity, unbelief, misbelief," lack of confidence or conviction.[14]

These words put things in a frightening perspective for me as a believer because of what we are really saying when we stress and allow disappointment or panic to set in, "God, I don't trust You," and "God, I don't believe You." That's also where we find ourselves getting into trouble trying to make things happen on our own, and when we get stuck in a mess, we call on God to help us. This reminds me of when we lived on a five-acre property, and our beloved pit bull Zeus was allowed to run the property unleashed because we trusted him not to go outside of the five acres. One day, my husband let him out, not realizing that a stray cat that always taunted Zeus had sauntered onto our property, and Zeus took off like a bolt of lightning to chase the cat. No matter how much my husband yelled for Zeus to stop and chased after him, Zeus did what he wanted and almost caught the cat (he was that swift) but got stuck in a thicket of our neighbor's bamboo trees. Poor Zeus didn't realize he couldn't make it through until half his body was stuck in the trees, and he began to cry for my husband to get him out. This is exactly how I behaved during this holiday season—I did want I wanted to, and when it didn't work out the way I wanted, I cried about it to God. I let the enemy make me feel as if I needed to make things happen that weren't happening with a "poor me, nothing ever works out for me" mentality, which are all lies from the enemy meant to distract us by encouraging us to give in to our flesh instead of staying the course that God has set before us. These are the moments that we need to go back to what God has promised, go back to His Word and see how believers in the Bible persevered and waited for the promise to come to pass by walking in obedience, and God rewarded them for it.

I was drawn to reading Psalm 112. I watched God reconfirm every promise He'd made to me and every word He gave me through the Holy Spirit. I know this to be true because as I read each corresponding scripture, God brought to my memory every promise and word He gave me relative to the passage I was reading. We must see ourselves as children holding our Father's hand and crossing a dangerous or perilous highway. Only God can see the danger up ahead, the pitfalls or traps, and what we ought to avoid. Only He knows when it's all clear and safe to cross. So, we must hold tightly to His hand and move when He moves or when He tells us to because our Father wants what is good for us. We need to be sensitive to the Holy Spirit, and I have to keep reminding myself that if the Holy Spirit keeps bringing me to an area of my life where I think I'm okay, then I know I'm not and need to recognize and acknowledge it. Remember: for God to heal us from something or set us free, we must first face or acknowledge the issue. For example, I am terribly impatient, and my children have said in the past that I have anger issues and road rage when I drive (which I vehemently deny!), but lately, I've found that every time I get on the road, I either get stuck in slow-moving traffic or stuck sandwiched between two cars going twenty miles below the speed limit. Now, when this happens, instead of yelling and getting upset at the person or speeding up trying to wiggle my way out, only to get stuck behind someone driving even slower, I ask myself, "What is the Holy Spirit saying to me that this keeps happening?" And now, instead of getting upset, I wait patiently, obey the speed limits, and be thankful that I get where I need to go safely. I'm reminded that it doesn't matter what other people think of me, but rather be concerned about what God thinks of me and how I treat others.

As Christians, we are to be a reflection of Christ. I could never imagine Jesus yelling at another person for driving too slowly and speeding around them, cutting them off; that's more a reflection of someone who is angry. We need to be concerned that God sees us and is well pleased with us.

November 11, 2021

Getting Rid of What Hurts

I was lying in bed this morning and leaned over to check my watch at 7:20 a.m.—another early morning. God wanted to talk to me, wanted me to spend time with Him. He brought a therapy session to my memory. All of the lessons that my counselor wanted to teach me and the tools she wanted to leave with me. I kept looking over at myself on the screen and didn't like how I looked at all during the video conference. (I'm always so critical of myself; "Why is that?" God asks...) At one point, I was talking to her and was using my hands, they seemed so huge on the screen, and my wrists looked so puffy that I put them down and hid them out of the camera's sight while I was talking. Then I was focused on my counselor's wrists; she was only a few years older than me; why didn't she have puffy wrists and fingers? *God, why did You make me this way?* I thought. Then I went down the list of things about myself that I was not happy with; these are the thoughts and questions that are the elephant in the room.

In my mind, I questioned what "fearfully made" means, and the Holy Spirit said to me, "With reverence," and gave me the answer! God's Word says that I am fearfully and wonderfully made (Psalm 139:14).

"Fearfully" comes from the Hebrew word *yārē*, meaning "to revere, respect, to be awesome." "Wonderfully," from the Hebrew word *pālā*, means "to cause to astound; to show oneself marvelous, be amazing, to do a marvelous work."[15]

How amazing is that? How awesome to know that God took His time and did a marvelous work—created you and me in the very image of Himself, and intends for us to live a life that is fulfilling and for His divine purpose. It makes me sad that in my selfishness and fleshly behavior, I've insulted God by putting down and criticizing His beautifully considered amazing design. The marvels of the human body are still an enigma to this very day because we have such an intelligent Creator that our minds cannot comprehend it. We question God and His love for us when we are self-deprecating or self-loathing or when we are critical of our physical appearance. He did not create us to be the same; even identical twins have unique personalities.

We are so busy looking at ourselves through the lens of a world that can make us feel inferior or less than others, not as pretty or talented as someone, but we are not called to be like the world. We need to start looking at ourselves through the eyes of Christ, who laid down His life for us and for our salvation. God didn't make us all to be alike, He made each of us with a special purpose in mind, so we need to replace those negative and comparative thoughts with God's Word!

"For we are His workmanship, created in Christ Jesus for good works, which God prepared beforehand that we should walk in them" (Ephesians 2:10)—not to walk in what the world says, not to walk according to the lies of the enemy, but to set aside our old ways, thoughts, or desires and follow after Christ. Each of us is valuable to God, and when He looks at us, He doesn't see our sin; God sees His Son (Galatians 2:20; Luke 12:7). There may be things in our lives or situations that we find difficult to overcome, but we have to use whatever tools we need to help us in areas that we have difficulty overcoming. Meaning to do what we need to do, such as getting professional counseling, seeking wise counsel, surrounding ourselves with Godly people, and God will do the rest. Jesus said, "Take heart, I have overcome the world" (John 16:33), meaning be strengthened or encouraged and walk out what God has for you; Jesus has suffered through every- and anything we could ever imagine, and He conquered them all for us so that through Him in His strength and courage; we can claim the victory. You must ask yourself what power the person or thing has over you. The only power the person or thing has is what you give it. Take back your God-given power and stand before your "Goliath" with the slingshot of God's truth in hand and take down that giant and cut off its head with the sword of the Spirit.

November 13, 2021

I had a hectic end to a rather stressful week today. I really need to be kinder to myself and understand that:

1. I don't need to know and do everything.
2. I don't have to fix everything.
3. It's okay to take a break or say no.
4. I don't have to be perfect!

A dear friend of mine asked me how I was doing this morning, and I told her I've felt overwhelmed and exhausted by what has been happening with my husband's health and how I've really had to suck it up and deal with his behaviors and find the grace to overlook transgressions when all I feel is the urge to scream and smash something. Thankfully I did not give in to those feelings, which speaks of growth and spiritual maturing. Not giving in to our fleshly desires even when we are tired or worn out is important to our spiritual growth. As I've mentioned before, the enemy will try to disrupt your sleep or stress you out in order to make you more susceptible to his lies and influences; but we must rise above and remember what God's

Word says in James 4:7 (AMP), "So submit to (the authority of) God. Resist the devil (stand firm against him) and he will flee from you." Give him no quarter, and he will take his foolishness elsewhere; that's not to say that he won't try again, but the more we humble ourselves to God, the better equipped we are (no matter how tired we may be) to resist the devil's tricks and schemes.

November 8, 2021

The Anniversary

Anniversaries are a strange animal: we celebrate and commemorate events that both bring us immense joy and incredible pain. Anniversary is described as the date on which an event took place in a previous year and comes from the Latin word *anniversarius*: "returning yearly."[16] We, humans, develop strange rituals, and I suppose that is how our human minds cope with certain events. Why do we feel the need to return each year to a place an event took place that made us sad? Such as the death of a loved one? I can remember the day my father passed away as clear as day; it's so etched in my memory because there was an incredible miracle that day that I know for sure God's hand was in. The day my father passed away, his partner called me to say that she had to take him to the hospital that Sunday night and that they had admitted him. She wanted me to know that he was now in the ICU and that his breathing was getting worse. My father had been diagnosed with ALS (Lou Gehrig's disease) the year before, and his health had been declining rapidly. My younger brother had surprised him with a visit that Sunday afternoon (I had planned to visit the following weekend to stay for a few days but never got the chance) and called me to say that Daddy had gotten worse since we had all seen him the week prior. That Monday, my father's significant other called to say that she had to take him to the ER on Sunday night because he had gotten even worse after my brother left, and they put him in intensive care. She promised to keep me updated as things progressed but stated she was waiting to speak with the doctors. I dropped everything and immediately reached out to my other siblings. While I was on the phone with my little sister giving her an update, my father's significant other called back. I connected the calls, and the three of us were on the line. The doctors had said there was nothing more that they could do.

In the midst of our pain and despair, God gave us a miracle. Before Daddy passed away, while I was on the phone talking to his partner and my little sister, my other brother and older sister from the Bahamas called, and we were now all on the same call. While we talked and tried to encourage each other, the nurse came out to say that my dad was getting even worse. The hospital staff was kind enough to allow the phone to be placed at Daddy's ear, and we were all able to speak to him and tell him how much we loved him. I didn't know that it would be the last time I spoke to my father because he passed while I was on my way to Orlando to see him. I cherish that last phone call and am so thankful every time I recall it because God was so gracious and knew how much it would mean to all of us. However, the events after and my bouts of illness are a blur.

Typically, we celebrate events that bring us joy and happiness, events that are important to us, such as a birthday or wedding anniversaries, but we seem to remember the day a person passes away. I've stopped commemorating that day because it makes me recall all of the pain and anguish we all went through during that very difficult time in my life. Instead, I choose to commemorate Daddy's birthday and draw on happy memories we made growing up and throughout my life: how he would tickle us instead of yell at us when we would stay up too late instead of going to bed when my sisters and I were younger, how he taught me how to play chess when I was nine or ten and stayed home sick from school. How my sister and I would go into his study as little girls and record ourselves singing, "Sweet brown sugar, I love you..." on his cassette tape recorder and the way he smiled when he played the tape back even though we weren't supposed to be on his desk. The memories that bring a smile to my face and that fill my heart with warmth are what I cling to. The Bible says in 1 Thessalonians 4:13–18 (NASB):

> But we do not want you to be uninformed, brethren, about those who are asleep, so that you will not grieve as do the rest who have no hope. For if we believe that Jesus died and rose again, even so God will bring with Him those who have fallen asleep in Jesus. For this we say to you by the word of the Lord, that we who are alive and remain until the coming of the Lord, will not precede those who have fallen asleep. For the Lord Himself will descend from heaven with a shout, with the voice of the archangel and with the trumpet of God, and the dead in Christ will rise first. Then we who are alive and remain will be caught up together

with them in the clouds to meet the Lord in the air, and so we shall always be with the Lord. Therefore comfort one another with these words.

Paul is telling us believers in Christ that while we grieve losing the people we love, we should not grieve as if we will never see them again but rather rest in the hope that Christ's resurrection gives us. Those who have passed away will be the first to meet Jesus in the air, and as a close friend of mine told me when I was in so much pain, Daddy is where all of us are trying to get to—in heaven with the Almighty.

So today, why, on the eve of our wedding anniversary, do I feel more like mourning than celebrating? I told my husband weeks ago that our anniversary doesn't mean what it once did, and what I explained was that everything that day and all that came after seemed all built on a lie. He married me because he felt he was put between a rock and a hard place and went along with the charade. He was never committed to this marriage, and sadly, when I said those very words to him, he did not deny it. Our marriage counselor said to me on the day of our first session that he obviously wanted to be married because he had stayed for twenty years. I'm sorry to say this, but I wanted to punch her in the face. Just because someone is too scared to let go doesn't mean they want to be where they are. He let anger, caused by the fact he was forced into a situation he didn't really want, saddled with the responsibility he felt he didn't ask for, fester into a bitterness that made him a resentful, spiteful, and selfish husband and father. He wanted to be responsible for himself, and I came along and upended his entire life. I read on a website that

anniversaries are an important part of life. They remind us of important events, both personal and cultural...It's a chance [to] reflect on a relationship or
cultural identity, to come together to remember a
person who has died, or to celebrate a joyous event.[17]

Whether it's the day they were born or died, it matters not;
either day reminds us that the loved one is no longer with us.
But in the case of a wedding anniversary, it brings so many
emotions to the surface; it makes one recall the vows made, the
shared memories, or in our case, it dredges up some very painful realities that I do not want to relive.

Vows that promise that two lives are joined as one, that we're
in it together, "I have your back no matter what may come"—so,
what do you do when none of those statements are ever true?
What do you do when you are reminded that you were the only
fool who believed the lie that day?

November 19 has certainly become a bitter taste in my
mouth. This is all the work of the enemy wanting us to wallow in the painful parts of life, remembering over and over
again like a recurring nightmare, the painful events to keep us
drowning in the darkness of constant pain; when God is right
there in the midst of it with a life preserver. The question you
must eventually ask yourself is: How much power am I going to
continue to give over to this thing? How much control will I let
it have over my life, over my happiness?

God told the Israelites to get up and keep moving, that they
had mourned for the appropriate time of thirty days, and that

it was time to move on. At some point, you have to give your-self over to the Potter's wheel and allow Him to make a new creation of you. We have to let God transform our minds and hearts by giving the burden over to Him and allowing Him to change how we see things and change how we let things affect us.

I look at my husband and see all of the work yet to be done and wonder if any of this is worth it. Will I ever see this marriage as the beautiful union that God intended it to be, or am I wasting my time and blocking the chance of meeting the one that God truly has for me because I deserve so much better? Then I remember that now, things are different because we're now including God in our relationship, which we did not do in the beginning and for nearly two decades. When God is in the midst of anything, He can do a new thing and take something once broken and make it whole. Only God can change an un-caring, selfish, compassionless person into a loving and car-ing, "all-in" kind of person; we just have to ask (pray), trust, and believe Him for it no matter how things may look—just as God told the Israelites after thirty days of grieving to get up and go, walk into the promises and the blessings He has in store for them. We must do the same: get up from the place of pain and mourning and walk into God's promises for us. I must re-member that as God is working on me and all my faults and wrong behaviors, He is doing the same with my husband––it just looks different.

Joshua 1 is a beautiful and heartwarming exchange where God, who knows His people are suffering and hurting, assures Joshua of His protection, love, and presence. He urges Joshua to remember His laws. He reminds Joshua of the promises He made to Abraham centuries prior.

God lovingly reminds me that we are in this together, that I need only trust Him, keep walking into the promises and plans He had for me before He formed me in my mother's womb, and that He will bring me into that promise of restoration. This is the promise that I need to remind myself of when I think about our anniversary date. The funny thing is that our original wedding date was November 20; we had to move the date because the church wasn't available, so we had to move the wedding up a day. Even though some of the things (wine goblets, cake knives) we bought had already been engraved with the twentieth.

But during these trials, I cling to God's word in Psalm 119:49–50, which says, "Remember the word to Your servant, Upon which You have caused me to hope. This is my comfort in my affliction, For Your word has given me life." Resting on God's promises brings hope to us all when we are going through afflictions, remembering that what He promises, He will indeed do. This is the hope, the only hope that we ought to cling to when the enemy comes in like a flood or rough seasons threaten to overtake us; we must hope and trust in the Lord.

November 19, 2021

God says, "Behold, I will do a new thing" (Isaiah 43:19); He is making something brand new, something unlike what we had before. Nothing is impossible for God, but He can only do as much in our lives as we believe He can. We must activate our faith and believe that all things are possible.

I have a friend who always told me, "If you believe like that, you'll receive like that," I choose to have radical faith and know and trust that I don't need to know the details, but I trust that all that God has promised will be done in my life exceedingly, abundantly, above all, I can "ask or think, according to the power that worketh in us" (Ephesians 3:20, KJV). I choose to hold God's hand in the darkness and to hold on and step out in faith, not knowing or seeing where I'm going but knowing and trusting it will be beautiful because God is leading me (Jeremiah 29:11).

November 20, 2021

I was listening to Acts 9 at the point where Ananias finds Saul, lays hands on him, baptizes Saul, and the scales fall from Saul's eyes. The Holy Spirit gave me a word when I got to the part where Saul goes out and starts preaching the good news that Jesus was the Messiah, the Son of God. The people started saying, "Aren't you the one who was persecuting and murdering Christians?" Essentially reminding him of who he used to be. The way the world tends to be the crucifixion chorus when those who are born again speak the only truth there is—God's. We are called to be not like the world, to come out from among them and not be like or live like them. You are set apart, so I need to remind myself, and you do as well, to remain firmly rooted in Christ, standing on the Word. We can be fearless and bold when speaking when God tells us to.

Sometimes God will test us to see if we stand on His Word no matter the attacks that may come our way. Will we stand up for what is written in Scripture, or will we cave under social pressure when no one else is standing with us? This is why we must ignore the whispers of the enemy, reminding us of who we used to be, and remember that we are baptized and made new.

November 21, 2021

Deep in the River, Low in the Valley

Several months ago, it was my turn to choose topics for our Bible study, and one of the topics that God put on my heart was Joseph. It was back in January, and I did not see it then, but it is so evident now why He chose Joseph as a topic. These past few months have been brutal. We have gone from one trial to another, and it has not stopped. I feel like I'm being tossed again beneath a tumultuous sea and can't find the surface, let alone come up for air. Some days I cry to God in the dark and ask, "Where are you? Why are you allowing me to go through this? I'm doing everything you're asking of me." Then I think of Joseph.

Joseph spent most of his adult life in a foreign land; he was sold into slavery, away from his family, and imprisoned without his parents' love; yet he persevered. Joseph suffered through many trials, and still, he remained faithful to God and grew in character. God not only blessed his obedience and showed him favor, but Potiphar and the pharaoh also showed him favor, and Joseph watched his dreams come to pass because of his faithful obedience to God.

Psalm 105:17–19 says, "He sent a man before them– Joseph––who was sold as a slave. They hurt his feet with fetters. He was laid in irons. Until the time that his word came to pass. The word of the LORD tested him." So, while what Joseph may have suffered seemed unfair, it was still preordained by God so that His ultimate plan to save his people from future famine would come to pass. Joseph's enslavement and seasons of affliction did not cancel God's plans for his life. Instead, he emerged well-equipped to handle the authority entrusted to him by the pharaoh and, most importantly, by God. In God's timing, once Joseph had gone through the testing and trials and proved his character worthy, God lifted him and made him the second most powerful man in Egypt.

Like Joseph, we will experience seasons of testing and afflictions. We must weather every storm with courage and allow the fiery furnace to burn away any impurities in our character that God is trying to rid us of or to make stronger those areas in need of fortification. If we run away from every challenge that comes our way, we will never be prepared for what God has in store for us. In life, we will face challenges; some will come from the enemy. If we are ill-prepared, they can be destructive. Our heavenly Father wants to prepare us for the rivers and valleys we may face in life. So, while I hate being in trying times, I welcome the storms because I know when they pass, I will come out on the other side with new weapons to wield in the next fight.

Jacob is another excellent example. Jacob's encounter with God is a perfect example of how our flesh wrestles against our spirit. Sometimes God has to break us to bless us, and we see this clearly when Jacob wrestles with God in Genesis 32:22–32.

When Jacob comes to the end of himself (the old man) and submits to God (the new man), he finally realizes that he must stop wrestling with God's will for his life to have peace. When we wrestle against God's will for our lives, we make things harder for ourselves and go through unnecessary struggles. Just as we all have some good days and some bad, Jacob did not always act as if he was made new or as if God had changed his name to Israel. God had to remind and reassure him shortly after their wrestling match of the promises that He made to him. We all must die to our flesh each day (2 Corinthians 4:16). God asks Jacob, "Who are you?" and it represents not just his calling but also that he is a new creation, the new man, and God is putting off the old man in us daily, and we need to surrender to Him. We must face who we used to be, just as Jacob did. Sometimes, we think it's Satan attacking us, but God uses the enemy's tools for our benefit. Each day as we surrender to God, He gives us new mercies and strength.

God is faithful even when we fall off course. He gave us His Word as a guide to show us not only how we should live but also to provide us with examples of how we should not. God wants us to see that despite our struggles, as we see many people throughout scripture stumble, it does not cancel His call on our lives. Throughout Scripture, Jacob is called Israel when he is operating in his new nature and Jacob when he is operating in his old, yet he still pressed on and trusted God. God chooses to accomplish His purpose through sinful people. He changes them and makes them new––provides them the power to overcome hardships. He proves faithful, and we must believe Him for His Word and works!

November 23, 2021

I've been feeling overwhelmed lately, rushed, too busy, and tired, and all of that has seemed to steal joy from me. I realized the reason for that is that I've allowed work and other things to push my time with God and to read the Bible in the background. I stress over my children and carry the burden of trying to follow through with marriage therapy and keep remembering to watch what I say and my behavior because God expects me to be the bigger person when it comes to others because I'm more spiritually mature (not perfect, but progressing along in my journey); I can't tell you how much that hurts—my flesh that is. How it makes you feel knowing that feelings should never lead us, the Holy Spirit should always. But when my husband says something that reminds me of the old him (making snide remarks) or is petty, I have to grit my teeth and bite my tongue until it bleeds. We all have habits that can sometimes be annoying to others, as none of us is perfect by any stretch of the imagination; therefore, we must treat each other with grace and give grace rather than annoyance and aggravation. Is this not what God does for all of us? We fall, do things that hurt Him, don't do what we are supposed to, and are sometimes selfish and self-serving, and yet He covers us with His grace and does not give us the punishment that we deserve. This is how we mature spiritually, by remembering that we too are sinners and need refinement and God's kindness, so who are we to begrudge another person the same?

November 25, 2021

Today is Thanksgiving Day, and I ask myself, "What am I thankful for?" I am thankful to be counted among those whom God chastises and corrects because that means He loves me! Hebrews 12:6 says, "For whom the LORD loves He chastens, And scourges every son whom He receives." The word "chasten" in Greek is *paideuw*, which means to "train up a child, i.e., educate, discipline (by punishment): chasten (-ise), instruct, learn, teach, or to correct with words."[18] Salvation and a personal relationship with our Lord and Savior are what I am most grateful for.

A parent who doesn't love his/her child fails to discipline him and lacks responsibility for the child. When you love your child, you want to correct wrong behaviors, set boundaries, and punish him or her or, when the child does wrong so that the child grows up with morals and a sense of right and wrong, spare him or her the pain of having society or the legal system do the correcting. We want what is best for our children and want to see them filled with joy. How much more does God want for us? To not be hurt by our bad decisions and wrong thinking?

Jeremiah 29:11 (NIV) is one of my favorite scriptures; it says, "'For I know the plans I have for you,' declares the Lord, 'plans to prosper you and not to harm you, plans to give you a hope and a future.'" God's plans are far better and more detailed than ours. God's promises are to give us hope; in this verse, God remembers His agreed promise of restoration—to bring what He promised to pass. But for this to happen, a covenant requires an agreement between two parties and understanding. We cannot be in agreement with the enemy (believing lies about ourselves, living our lives the way we want to, and ignoring God's Word) by listening to the insecure parts of our flesh that tell us to feel hurt by a perceived slight or to hang onto a grudge or to seek retribution for a wrong; this can hinder any agreement we may have with God because light and darkness cannot share the same space (2 Corinthians 6:14) and we cannot serve two masters.

Jesus says in His Sermon on the Mount that "no one can serve two masters. Either you will hate the one and love the other, or you will be devoted to the one and despise the other. You cannot serve both God and money" (Matthew 6:24, NIV). At some point, both masters will make demands of you that are in direct opposition to each other, so you are walking either in the light or the darkness, not both.

We have to be humble enough to ask the difficult questions that will help us grow. Last night I asked God what thing I am struggling with that I need to address, and He responded, "Your insecurities"—the part of me that makes me feel disrespected when I ask my husband a question, and he turns and says, "What?" with a foolish questioning look on his face. Or the part of me that wants to snap back when someone makes a joke at my expense, whether it's in fun or not, and hold onto the slight all day long, stewing in my hurt feelings. I know that I cannot carry these insecurities and petty grievances with me when God takes me to places and levels where I cannot go on my own. Think about the people we would turn away from Christ, behaving this way when we are supposed to be the image of Christ and the light of the world that draws others to God.

The day before that, God took me to two scriptures, 2 Kings 20:12, where King Hezekiah shows off his treasures to the Babylonian visitors, giving in to worldly pride, and 2 Samuel 24, where King David counts his troops against the advice of his commander, thereby taking credit for success and power he was given from God. Both instances stemmed from pride, and somewhere twisted up in pride's tangled web, in some cases, are insecurities. If I am being honest, parts of me would be saying, "Hah! Look at me now! You talked about me and put me down but look where I am and what I have!" That's a dangerous road we go down when we let Satan whisper nasty things in our ears, speaking to the insecure parts of us that need to be puffed up. A weapon the enemy uses against us time and time again and causes us to sin against God by acting out of pride and taking credit for things that only through God's power were made possible. The fact that God takes time, out of billions of people in the world, to share something with His daughter so that she can be healed and made whole demonstrates a divine love that I find so incredibly amazing. He sees our struggles and wants to see us set free of these entanglements so that when these attacks come (remember: God tests us but never tempts us), whether on a small or major level, we are firmly planted in Christ, filled with God's Word, following the guidance of the Holy Spirit and equipped to weather any storm. We become shipwrecked when we allow the enemy to climb aboard and steer the vessel. Remember, we have a crafty and smart enemy who studies us and whose sole goal is to kill, steal and destroy. Why would we knowingly invite someone like that into our lives? That's what we're doing when we give in to our feelings and our flesh. When that wrong voice in your head says, "Pay him back because look what he did you!" or, "Remember what she said to you? Say something that would cut her deeply," or, "Remember what they did to you? Don't help them out!"—this is the enemy steering the ship and getting you further and further away from shore. Just as God shares His throne with no one, He will not share a stage with the enemy, so either we follow and believe God, or we follow and believe the enemy.

God is preparing me for something far bigger than my mind can imagine or fathom, so I must be in lockstep with Him, not entertaining and in concert with the enemy. God cares about our personal relationship with Him, our obedience, reading and studying His Word, our spiritual growth, and that we follow His plans and purposes for our lives.

November 26, 2021

Today, my husband finally got the scheduling of the marriage counseling somewhat sorted out. I am so annoyed, well, a bit heartbroken at the disregard and lack of consideration he has for me, and it doesn't take much or take long for his annoyance with me to turn into passive-aggressive, spiteful disregard. Like he withholds his affection and consideration when I say or do something to make him upset or mad. I have been intentional about considering him and being compassionate and considerate toward him even when he doesn't deserve it. For example, complimenting him consistently about how he cleaned up the garage (words of affirmation which I've learned is his main love language), making the bed and not keeping score or being petty about it being my turn, taking his clothes out of the dryer and folding them without him asking, washing dishes that everyone else left in the sink and putting stuff away because I know that it annoys him when it's not done. I hold my tongue when he says something snarky or something I find hurtful instead of saying something nasty out of anger; I keep hearing God's Word: "Be angry and do not sin; do not let the sun go down on your anger" (Ephesians 4:26) and Psalm 4:4 again, "Be angry, and do not sin. Meditate within your heart on your bed, and be still" so not let my anger turn into actions that are considered sinful to God. Instead, I try to focus on God and what He wants me to do and let the Holy Spirit be my guide because my first reaction is to give in to my feelings, which is being carnal—lashing out is all carnal. So, I remind myself, as Paul did to the church of Ephesus, that we have become new creatures through Christ's work on the cross; the old (who we used to be) is no more. So, I must behave as a mature individual in order to grow and mature as a Christian, which is why I do not react when my husband makes fun of me because it feels like it comes from an ugly place. This is why we must submit to the Holy Spirit's guidance (Ephesians 4:23–24). During this process, I have realized that my mind is being renewed, that more often than not, I turn away wrath with gentle words (oh, trust me, sometimes it's through gritted teeth) and behaviors. I don't always succeed at it, but I can honestly see how I've changed, and God's not done working on me.

Yesterday was Thanksgiving, and my husband was upset with me the whole day. I didn't react, though deep down, it hurt because I was being obedient, treating him with grace and compassion, yet he still felt comfortable treating me as if I didn't matter and like an afterthought or taking his frustrations out on me. The night before, he was visibly upset for two reasons:

1. I think he's harboring resentment because his plans for Thanksgiving did not line up with mine because we had already made plans with my oldest son and daughter-

in-law. It's as if he's reverted to his way of "punishing" me when I don't give him what he wants.

2. Perhaps he feels that I'm forcing him to do what I want.

I feel as though I am on an island all by myself, doing the work needed to lift my family before God and restore my marriage, but I feel I'm doing it alone. Like my husband is off doing what works for him and what feels good to him. My mind knows that God is working behind the scenes, but my heart is still breaking watching him do and say some of the same old things and do an awfully poor job of pretending he's okay and everything is good.

We're about to start couples counseling, and I have no idea what I want from him. What can he give me? What can I trust him to provide for me? I had hoped, as our anniversary came (and went), that he would at least see that we needed to start over—an actual "do-over" of our relationship. All he does is complain and gripe about the things he feels directly affect him.

I've been forced to care for myself and provide what I needed for myself for so long that I have no clue what I want or need from him as a husband. How sad is that? I can't begin to say; I mean, I have a difficult time asking him to get or do anything for me without feeling the urge to offer him money or do something in return so that I don't "owe" him or have to listen to him bring it up. That's always been the environment he's fostered in our relationship, even in the gift-giving: "Do you know how much I spent?" or "Do you know what that cost me?" Oh, and a big one: "What are you going to do for me?" "Who's paying for this?" "Are you going to pay for half?" To me, all of these questions scream, "I don't care about you, so I'm not taking care of you!"

When Daddy was here with us, he was the man in my life who cared about and for me, the man who provided for me. Now that he's gone to be with the Lord, God has filled the void and continues to provide as He always has! So, where does my husband fit in as my provider here on the earth? I can't be the only one constantly compromising, the only one being considerate, the only one thinking before acting or speaking. It's not sustainable. Thank God it's not up to me; it's God who can and will do it.

I'm not able to share intimate things with my husband because we are rebuilding trust in our relationship. We drive in the car in silence; he has music blasting, which says to me that he doesn't want to talk to me. This makes me question exactly what we have in common.

I've also come to realize that we often expect things from other people that they are incapable of providing and that only God alone can give us. We look to other people (or sometimes things) to fill some of the gaps within us, to patch together the pieces inside of us that are broken, and there is no person on this earth who can make us whole. Relationships require work and a give and take where both parties are all in, but what makes a marriage whole is when God is at the center of it, and we both trust Him to give us the things that we cannot get from our spouse.

Yesterday my husband asked me to help him take the Christmas decorations down from the attic in the garage so that it turned into him doing more of what he wanted—to move items out of the garage and throw them out. Never once caring if I was okay or what I thought. For some reason, he behaves territorial and marks the garage off as his personal space. Moving things that he considered not his and putting them inside our tiny living quarters and announcing that it's not going back into the garage. A garage that is considered half mine, a garage overrun with his stuff, and he complained over "all of my stuff that's taking up space" in the garage that he wants out, claiming that most of the junk in there was mine, which I had long said wasn't true, but it took someone else coming by and saying the very same thing for my husband to admit it. So, he then brought down containers full of some Christmas decorations, thirteen boxes in total, and only one actually had the decorations that we intended to put up. When I asked him where the stuff was to go, he suggested they could stay in the living room and proceeded to pile everything up near the only window in our living room. When I complained about it, he suggested putting the container on the patio in the pool area, which looked like a complete mess because he had containers stored out there for months.

When he asked me this morning what we were doing today, I told him the containers could not remain in the living room because they looked too cluttered and hindered access to the one living room window. He hesitated and said, "Let me think about it"; his response took me by surprise because it felt like I was in a dictatorship where I had to ask permission. Then I realized that these petty grievances and slights are exactly how the enemy comes in and creates division in a home, and as Jesus says in the Gospel of Mark 3:25, "And if a house be divided against itself, that house cannot stand." So, the question we must ask when situations like these arise is how long do we continue to give up ground and allow the enemy to play *Wreck-it Ralph* in our lives and in our families?

God reminded me that "there are many plans in a man's heart. Nevertheless the Lord's counsel—that will stand" (Proverbs 19:21). So, it is God who controls the end result.

November 30, 2021

Philippians 4:6–7 says,

> Be anxious for nothing but in everything by prayer and supplication, with thanksgiving, let your requests be made known to God; and the peace of God, which surpasses all understanding, will guard your hearts and minds through Christ Jesus.

These past two weeks have been such a test for me. In my heart, deep down in my spirit, I know that God has me covered, and no matter what, His promises for me—to me—will come to pass. I have to admit that after dealing with a plumbing issue that was causing everything to back up in the bathtubs, toilets, and sinks—and we were unable to use the washing machine; we were denied a HELOC loan and then had to pay to have the septic tank drained to try to alleviate the problem—I was completely overwhelmed. Then my husband came up to me, asking me, "What do we do now?" And his main concern was any negative financial impact on him personally. I was so overwhelmed with everything, not to mention the burden of dealing with my husband's old behaviors, but God has a way of putting things in perspective when we listen to the Holy Spirit who dwells within each of us. When it comes to the things of God, we must close our fleshly eyes so that our spiritual eyes can open and see what God is truly saying to us. When we see from the flesh, things become distorted. Sometimes we are so focused on what we want that we miss the great things God has in store for us when He closes a door and prepares to open a door to something far better because we are so busy stressing over the mess before us. We must keep our eyes fixed on where our help comes from.

December 1, 2021

The Holy Spirit reminded me that not everyone who comes dressed in white is an angel of light and that I must test every spirit because darkness often cloaks itself in light. Issues we ignore and don't want to deal with and choose to hide away can bubble up in parts of our lives at the most inopportune times and in the worst possible situation. Going through all of these troubles makes me feel as if I'm seven years old again and at a pool playdate where a girl, who did not know I could not swim, pushed me into the deep end of the pool, and for what seemed like a lifetime, I sank to the bottom of the pool, drowning before anyone noticed and pulled me out; gasping for air, lungs burning, my eyes rolling back in my head, the weight of the water too much—that's how I feel. As if I'm being crushed, and it doesn't feel good; it's hard; it hurts, and I'm going through mentally and physically taxing trials, but God is not done because there is still much work to do in me. When the enemy attacks you mentally and taxes you physically and emotionally, the natural thing to do is run away from it as Gideon did when he hid in the winepress, a device where grapes are trampled, pressed, and squeezed to draw out the goodness that makes the sweetest of wines. I know there is a purpose to it all and see it even more so dealing with my husband's health issues, pressure from work to perform, dealing with issues at the house, and my children going through issues that, as I write, I feel so much turmoil roiling around inside of me like I'm being tossed around in a tumultuous sea of hurt and pain. I don't know which way is up and am just floating, waiting for God to give me direction, for Him to throw me a life preserver, as I know that I'm in His hands and He's there with me, and yet still I second guess everything because when we're in the fire, the enemy creeps about in the fringes throwing his jeers and lies. Being in a job that I loathe, it's easy to give in to complaining and anger and wonder why God hasn't delivered me yet. It's easy for us to miss what God is doing when we're in the midst of our pain, easy to lash out and miss what God is teaching us where He has us planted. Perhaps it's to learn perseverance, or maybe to learn how to submit to authority, and most importantly, to learn how to trust Him no matter what things look or feel like. So, while I'm going through this pressing, the question I'm asking myself is, "God, what are You showing me? What am I supposed to learn?" instead of trying to get out of it. Instead, I need to be obedient and wait for God to move.

December 2, 2021

When we find ourselves between a rock and a hard place, we need to realize that the God we serve is strong and mighty in battle, undefeated! Unbeatable: there is none like Him! The scene from the movie Troy comes to mind: in the first battle scene, Achilles comes storming through the front lines, leaps in the air, falls on the giant warrior killing him with a single sword thrust, and screams, "Is there no one else (brave enough to face me)?" We could search the world over and find none like our God, so why then do we insult Him by instead taking matters into our own hands when things go awry or don't work out? We're the ones screaming, "Is there no one else who can help me?" instead of turning to the One who is strong and mighty in battle and who is able to slay every enemy with one swift stroke! Psalm 31:17 (NIV) says, "The righteous cry out, and the LORD hears them; he delivers them from all their troubles." Which means God should be our first resort and not our last. There are many examples throughout scripture where God answered when His people cried out to Him. The disciples cried out to Jesus in the midst of the storm, and Jesus calmed the raging seas; blind Bartimaeus cried out to Jesus for mercy, and his sight was restored; Elijah cried out for the dead boy, and God revived him. When we cry out to God, He is faithful to deliver His people. It shows humility and demonstrates complete dependence upon Him.

December 4, 2021

It's been a struggle the past two and a half weeks—attacks all around and me allowing the enemy to run amuck in my mind, causing me to miss God's direction, His messages, and get my wires crossed. Then I stopped spinning my wheels and reminded myself whose I am by going to the Word, going before the throne in prayer, and giving all control over to the Holy Spirit. When we take our hands off of a situation and give it to God, an amazing thing happens, and the weight of worry lifts.

December 6, 2021

Riding in the car today on my way to pick up a gift for my niece from Target, I had the radio off and just drove in silence because sometimes it's a good way for me to clear my head and shut out all the negative noise. I must be honest, sometimes it's tough waiting on God and being obedient in the midst of trials, but in the end, there is no place I'd rather be.

As I sat questioning whether I was getting anything out of this couples counseling, wondering if it's having any effect on my husband, as I don't see any changes in him, God reminded me that the therapist isn't the one that's going to change my husband, his bad habits and how he treats me, or how he views our family; but God reminds me that it is He who gives a man a heart of flesh and the Holy Spirit within who makes the change. Counseling is meant to be a tool, and it is God who brings about the kind of change that a relationship needs to grow and become healthy. So the lesson for me here is to be obedient and keep up with our counseling appointments and leave the rest in God's hands. This is where I realized that we don't need to know what we need because God knows exactly what we need and the right time to give it to us. It's an awesome place to be when you can let go of a chaotic situation and allow God to do mighty work in the midst, lay your burdens down, and rest in that peaceful comfort of being in the hands of the Almighty. So, I need to let God be God and be obedient even when things don't seem to be working out; keep pressing on and doing the right thing even when it seems like nothing is happening because God is true to His Word and does everything He promises to do!

December 7, 2021

We often believe falsely that the enemy plays fair, that when we're going through turbulent times or trials or moments of testing that he'll only take his hits one shot at a time. Well, that's where we go wrong. As Tom Cruise's character in the movie *A Few Good Men* said, "And the hits just keep on coming." One right after the other, sometimes all at the same time, like a barrage of bullets or a hail of arrows aimed right at you to take you out. While you're going through it, the urge to give up is so strong it almost seems like a relief to give in, but that would be giving in to the enemy. That would mean being a friend to the world and at enmity with God (James 4:4). If we must be in agreement with someone (we can only choose one of the two), we must choose God every time. The enemy is not more powerful than the ever-living God (see excerpt below from *Strong's Concordance*).

We cannot be in agreement with the enemy when it comes to the things of the spirit. We must drench ourselves in the

Word of God to remind ourselves of the God we serve, a God who has never lost a battle, the God of Abraham, Isaac, and Jacob who keeps His promises. He uses these times of testing and trouble to remind us of the power we wield through Christ Jesus to defeat the enemy, demolish strongholds, and cast down every false suggestion of the enemy. Do you know what that means? The enemy can only suggest things to us; he has no power whatsoever other than the power we give up to him. Every lie he tells us, "You're not worthy," "No one really loves you," "You're a victim, poor you," we must call out and go to the Word of God that tells us we must be sober and vigilant. "Be alert and of sober mind. Your enemy the devil prowls around like a roaring lion looking for someone to devour" (1 Peter 5:8, NIV), or other translations say, "watch out" or "be watchful."

> Therefore, put on the full armor of God, so that when the day of evil comes, you may be able to stand your ground, and after you have done everything, to stand. Stand firm then, with the belt of truth buckled around your waist, with the breastplate of righteousness in place, and with your feet fitted with the readiness that comes from the gospel of peace. In addition to all this, take up the shield of faith, with which you can extinguish all the flaming arrows of the evil one. Take the helmet of salvation and the sword of the Spirit, which is the word of God.
>
> Ephesians 6:13–17

"Standing strong in faith" means believing in God and believing His Word to be true. Arming and equipping ourselves with the weapons to defeat the enemy (an already defeated foe) means knowing the Word of God. Not just reciting or memorizing it but getting revelation, a deeper meaning to it by spending time with God.

I know it's easier said than done because, many a time, I've been exhausted by what's going on around me, and everything happening to me becomes so overwhelming that I don't know what to do. This happened to me a week or so ago: I felt as if my marriage was regressing; my husband was falling back into old habits; I was, too—by letting things he was saying or doing frustrate and anger me. My boss was putting pressure on me to "perform better" and bring my numbers up, our drain field was not functioning, and sewage came up into the house, so we had to get the septic pumped out and try to find the $6,000 to repair it, then my daughter and I went to the dentist, and we both needed dental work and cleanings to the tune of $1,700; my paycheck seemed to be getting smaller and smaller, and the light around me seemed to be getting dimmer and dimmer, and I'd begun to let despair start to rear its ugly head. But can I share something with you? God put it on my heart, and the Holy Spirit nudged me to read God's Word and worship. It sounds strange and seems difficult considering what I was going through, but obedience to God is key to deliverance and breakthrough; there was a weight that lifted from my shoulders and a happiness/joy that set in because the Creator of the universe had me in the palm of His hand. His Word reminded me that He will set a table before me in the presence of my enemies, that my cup will overflow with blessings, that in this crushing season, He will bring forth something beautiful... pressed down, shaken together, and running over. That trials are necessary for strengthening our faith and drawing us closer to Him. These trials build us up so that we have the spiritual strength (like exercising our muscles for maximum strength and endurance) to tackle the trials and tribulations that come at us throughout our lives. This reminds me of raising children: when they are little, their needs and issues are small and manageable. We teach them as they grow and equip them to handle challenges. As they get older, their problems become more challenging, yet they grow in their ability to handle them. Our growth in Christ should be such that we are better equipped to handle life's trials.

December 9, 2021

The End of Individual Therapy

I had a good session today where we discussed the way forward and how I need to be mindful of what my husband is dealing with when we begin our couples therapy: to be considerate and like Christ, allowing others grace. It's easy when we are wounded by the acts of others and are innocent victims; we tend to forget that we, too, have issues to work out and certainly a part to play in what happened and what happens next. While I don't blame myself for what my husband did, I, too, have baggage that needs to be unpacked and dealt with.

I have a key lime and Meyer lemon tree that was killed (or so I thought) during a severe cold snap here in Florida where the temperature dropped down into the thirties; yet when spring came, it managed to sprout green leaves from the dried-up twigs, from those leaves blossoms surprisingly grew after my husband told me it wouldn't bear fruit because I kept it inside our screened in patio around the pool area, and according to him, it would never be pollinated. I disagreed because we purchased it from our local Home Depot in the garden section, which was mostly screened in also. That lime tree had everything it needed programmed into its roots and hidden inside its branches, waiting for the right time to become laden with healthy fruit. We need to be like my little lime tree; despite the battering we sometimes take, we need to let God bring out what He's put deep down in us since we were formed in our mother's womb. The other side of that potted lemon/lime tree was dried up and looked like spindly twigs, yet this tree had the promise of bearing fruit buried deep inside! Later on that spring, we had heavy rains and battering winds that assaulted my little lime tree, destroying many of the new buds. This happened several times, and I was concerned there would be nothing left, yet here I was, picking her fruits by the handful well into December with many more left to ripen. My point here is that we don't know what God has planted inside of each of us, seeds of greatness that, when planted in the right soil (in Christ), under the right conditions, can reap a bountiful harvest. Staying rooted and planted in Christ is that good soil, feeding ourselves the Word of God as the perfect nutrients for our growth. Staying connected to the true Vine (Jesus Christ) ensures that no matter the battering rain or destroying wind, we will endure and bear much fruit like my little lime tree—she may have been bruised but not broken, crushed but not utterly destroyed—this is what God does in our lives. He breathes life into barren, dry places. We need to prophesy to these places in our lives and speak life over them and believe it and watch the hand of God move. God's Word says in 2 Corinthians 4:8–10,

We are hard pressed on every side, yet not crushed; we are perplexed, but not in despair; persecuted, but not forsaken; struck down, but not destroyed, always carrying about in the body the dying of the Lord Jesus, that the life of Jesus also may be manifested in our body.

According to Strong, the word "forsaken" in Greek is *enkataleipō*, meaning "let remain over, or to desert: forsake, leave."[19] Though we may be afflicted and suffer setbacks in life, God will never allow these things to destroy us. But we must remember whose hand controls the storm, draw on our strength through Christ, and not give in to despair. As we are followers of Christ who believe in the death, burial, and resurrection, Jesus tells us that in our lives, we will have trials; however, God is the One who controls it all and uses these times of testing and trouble to strengthen His children and to grow our faith.

We must know that we may go through many trials (some minor, some great), but we are not left to our own devices because the Creator, the Good Shepherd, is leading His sheep beside still waters and restores our souls, just as He did for Paul and many others in the Bible.

December 10, 2021

This morning, God placed the theme of distraction on my heart. A distraction is defined as "that which distracts, divides the attention, or prevents concentration; to draw away or divert, as the mind or attention" (Dictionary app). Anything that gets in the way of our time with God or interrupts that time is a distraction that, if we allow it to become a habit, can be detrimental to us spiritually. First Timothy 4:8 (NIV) reads, "For physical training is of some value, but godliness has value for all things, holding promise for both the present life and the life to come." So, our focus should be on spiritual training and discipline that will benefit our lives in the long run.

The Lord is faithful to warn us when we seem to get off track or when we're doing something detrimental to our spiritual health that can be damaging to our relationship with Him. So many things in our natural lives (or rather everything) are tied to our spiritual lives and our relationship with God.

When I look at my husband, I can tell immediately when he's struggling spiritually because he begins to look ill; he struggles physically. I always wondered why I get up in the morning and sometimes am really tired; I rarely take anything to help me sleep; yet, he takes a medication to sleep, yet he seems not to get enough sleep as he always wakes up tired. From speaking to him, I can hear the lingering of his worldly views and old, worldly behaviors that resurface when he's under pressure. Kind of where I was at the very beginning of my walk (i.e., still holding onto political world views, being judgmental, etc.), indicating that he's not yet fully given himself over to God for refining.

This is what comes from believing you're a victim and you can't do anything about it because that's "just the way I am," is your mantra. When we are born again, we become new creations through Christ's work on the cross. How then can we still be "the way we are" if we are made new? The two cannot be true. God's Word says, "Therefore if any man be in Christ, he is a new creature: old things are passed away; behold all things have become new" (2 Corinthians 5:17). As we profess our faith in Jesus Christ being the only source of our salvation, we must also believe and realize that we not only have a new name and wear new garments but also have a new heart and a new character or new attributes. God's grace is what makes extraordinary changes in our souls, and when that takes place, old things (old thought processes, doctrines, and attitudes) are dead and gone and should exist no more. As a renewed soul with a new moral character, and new thought processes, everything must become, does become new. Our circle of influence, how we think, and how we operate should reflect that newness. It is a daily struggle sometimes when the pressures of life seem to weigh on us, but that is why God calls us to praise and worship. That is where we find respite and the strength to win the battle between flesh and spirit.

December 12, 2021

This morning, I asked God to show me or tell me what scripture I should read. Proverbs was on my mind this week, and I have marriage counseling this evening. I grabbed my Bible, and the Holy Spirit put Proverbs 31 in my heart! "A Wife of Valor," verses 11, 15, 16, 17, 20–22, 24–29, 31, especially stood out to me! So, I began a Bible study on it.

I realized that, in the natural, I have a difficult time, or should I say a hard time, getting rid of broken things or things I no longer have a use for. Like our curved TV with only half of the screen working—I cringed when my husband said he was taking it to the dump. Why do I have such a hard time letting go of things? I mean, they are just "things." Or is it indicative of something deeper? I am, as I grow in my walk with Christ—with God—learning how to let go of things that don't matter, how not to say things I shouldn't, how to give others grace and realize everyone is battling something in one form or another. It is so important to remember that God does not condemn; the

enemy does. We need to pray for others when they are struggling and treat us poorly or "offend" us. We need to be more
concerned with offending God!

So, I am learning to let go of things, let go of old behaviors,
let go of old habits, and let go of old tools that I once whipped
out so eagerly that are not only damaging to me but to others.
Like when I allow my feelings to take over when my husband
says or does something to me that I find inconsiderate or rude
(i.e., I washed all of his clothes by hand when we could not use
our washing machine so he wouldn't have to or stress out about
it because of our plumbing issue and he still complained that I
allowed his shirts to wrinkle). So, this Bible study was all about
what God needed me to learn. When I think of a woman of val-
or or bravery, I think of Esther, who put the needs of her people
before her own. She was teachable, exercised wisdom, accepted
wise counsel, and acted with courage.

God makes us wait on the promise because we need to grow
in our faith and mature in our relationship with Him. If we get
the promise too soon, we will lose it, or it will destroy us. Think
of Esther and all of the preparation she had to go through before she went to the palace. It was all to prepare her for what
God was going to use her to do.

December 13, 2021

It's amazing how when we are in God's waiting room, if we're being honest with ourselves and we truly self-reflect, we will see why God has us waiting. Constant self-reflection is a good way to remain humble and allows us to realize that there are things within us that we need to work on and fix because I've noticed with me that old habits creep in and resurface when pressure comes, I'm frustrated, or I've got a lot going on, old bad habits pop up in my beautiful garden like nasty little weeds. So we have to really self-reflect and be honest with ourselves and ask, "What is it that God wants me to work on?" or "What is it that God wants to reveal to me?" "What is within me that He wants to rid me and cleanse me of and set me free from so that He can give me the blessing He has in store for me?"

December 15, 2021

It's easy to think in a crushing season that God is far off and that He's distant, He does not hear you, is not paying attention to you, or that you're by yourself, but God is never closer than when we're going through a difficult time. He's working behind the scenes, growing our faith in every season; He's never more present than when we are going through struggles. He shows up in so many ways that we often ignore. A video on YouTube that may pop up on your feed with a pastor that has a message that speaks to you or random phone calls from a friend that prompts you to talk about something that's been weighing heavy on your heart or a daily devotional that has a message that really resonates with you; these are the many different ways that God speaks. He's omnipresent and can do anything the way He chooses. We just have to incline our ears and listen. We have to be in tune with the Holy Spirit to be able to pick up on when God is really speaking to us. It doesn't necessarily have to be in an audible voice, with which sometimes He may speak, but He speaks in so many different ways, and if we're paying attention, we'll catch them each and every time.

God is so incredibly amazing in how He deals with us! Yesterday He reminded me through a dear friend that, as believers walking with Christ, we may oftentimes have people in our close inner circle who may not be as spiritually mature or who may not be on the same level as we are, so we must be careful not to be in lockstep with that person and have wisdom about the conversations we have with that person and be more sensitive to the Holy Spirit when interacting with the person. Now, this is in no way a slight against any person, but rather a lesson that we all grow at different rates spiritually and have different experiences.

There is a reason why strong pastors have "elders" from whom they seek "wise counsel": strong and mature Christians who have spiritual authority and are men or women of wisdom (1 Timothy 3:1–7 and Titus 1:6–9). So, rather than confiding in such a person, I must instead seek prudent counsel lest I stunt my growth spiritually.

December 16, 2021

God is so amazing, and I can't say that enough because we sometimes forget how truly amazing He is! Jesus said that, in this world, we will have trouble and that we have to take heart because He has overcome the world. I absolutely love that: whatever we may go through, we can trust that we already have the victory because Jesus has already defeated it! God's Word in Psalm 34:19 reads as: "Many are the afflictions of the righteous, But the LORD delivers him out of them all," meaning once we've gone through the purging, purification, instruction, obedience, and whatever improvements God is perfecting in us; God delivers us. It's a testing of our faith, ridding us of anything that may hinder God's plans for our lives. I've realized that when we fail the test, God will put us back in the classroom to take the course again until we pass the test or learn the lesson. For me, that looks like putting me in situations that can rile me up, annoy me, or test my patience. I have been known to go from zero to angry quickly, and though I've gotten better and no longer curse or show my anger, the perfect combination of all the wrong ingredients in a situation can cause those old habits to surface. You know it's something you need to let the

Holy Spirit purge you of when you're flipping people off in your dreams, and not just one finger but two. Or when my husband asks to drive my car when I ask him to do a favor for me, and my immediate reaction is to say no and to have the Holy Spirit say to me, "But he's doing you a favor!" What a beautiful thing it is (albeit painful) to have God take time to remind us or show little old me what He needs me to correct so He can use me; it is absolutely incredible to me! We should all have a reverence for the fact that we are each so important to God that He takes the time with each and every one of us to teach us how to enter through the narrow gate (Matthew 7:13–14). He loves each of us too much to have us walk in error.

A dear friend of mine said to me once that the amount of opposition we face matches the level of calling on our lives. So, when we find ourselves going through challenges, we know that God's purpose is to use them for our good (Romans 8:28). To either bless us or bless someone else. I never thought that when I fell in love with writing at a very young age that it was for such a time as this! That my love for writing would be for the purpose of sharing my experience with others to set someone free who may be having the same struggles as I am. It's difficult to grasp how God will allow us to experience difficult situations that we can find no answers for; until we realize how much our testimony of how He brought us out of the depths of despair can set another person free! Others need to see how God did a mighty work in our lives, so it kindles hope within them, so they are drawn to Christ's light that shines through us.

It's difficult dealing with matters of the heart: betrayal, abuse, failure; for some reason, I would rather deal with any other situation than with a matter that could potentially hurt me emotionally or have the potential to break my heart. Imagine how God feels when He sees us going down a path that would lead to the exact kind of heartbreak. We all want to love and be loved, and there are times when that love doesn't look like what we'd envisioned or dreamed of, so there may be some embarrassment there or maybe a reluctance to let people know things aren't as they seem. But what if you could spare someone else the heartache? What if you could help someone else navigate the turbulent waters? That's what I found myself facing. At first, I grappled with how to hide my identity when writing this book because I wouldn't want people who know me to know; then, it switched to I'll get through it, to who cares as long as someone is being set free? That's God! All God. God equips those He calls to a specific purpose. Look at Gideon, Moses, Jeremiah, and others in the Bible. They all felt ill-equipped for what God called them to do, but we see through their stories that God gave them exactly what they needed to accomplish exactly what He asked of them. To the human eye and with our human minds, it seems impossible; but when God's hand is on it, all things are possible. When Moses was called to go before the pharaoh to plead for the freedom of God's people and to lead the nation of Israel out of Egypt, he questioned God's plan. He went through every reason why he was not qualified, the way we often do when God calls us or wants to use us for a specific purpose. What Moses hadn't realized, and we don't either, is that everything that happens in our lives is either part of God's plan or something God weaves into His plan. Even our mistakes He will use to achieve His plans and purposes for our lives.

When we get tired of arguing with God, running and hiding from what He's asking us to do, our forty-year season in the wilderness comes to an end.

December 20, 2021

This is the weekend before Christmas, and I have had many disappointments. I had hoped and prayed for a perfect holiday with all of my loved ones gathered together in one place, but it was not to be. I've realized that God doesn't always give us what we ask for when we ask for it because He always has something far better in store, something that may be far off but still much better. Ephesians 3:20 says, "God is able to do exceedingly, abundantly, and above all, you could ever ask, imagine, or think, according to His power at work in you. To Him be the glory." So, I know and wait with an expectant heart on the Lord because He always does what His Word says He will do.

Then I was searching scripture to find Ephesians 3:20, and instead, Zechariah 10:1 caught my eye and settled into my spirit for a very good reason. I don't know about anyone else, but this is one of the ways that God speaks to me. He gives me a scripture that illuminates exactly what He wants to tell me at any given time. It's the most incredibly amazing thing! The scripture reads, "Ask the LORD for rain in the springtime; it is the LORD who sends the thunderstorms. He gives showers of rain to all people, and plants of the field to everyone" (Zechariah 10:1, NIV). When we weather life's storms, soldiering on through some of the toughest times, it is God who brings the shower of blessings. We reap the bountiful harvest, but we must acknowledge God's hand in all situations, whether they are times of challenge and strife or times of great blessings.

I also learned this week that when we let go of past hurts and things that people have done to us and let God do a work in us, that's when real healing begins, and God is able to do His best work. We must first give up all control and fully *submit*, which means "to give over or yield to the power or authority of another,"[20] so we need to give up our control over a situation, relinquish what we think things should be, and let God do His work in us.

December 23, 2021

"I will give you a new heart and put a new spirit within you; I will take the heart of stone out of your flesh and give you a heart of flesh" (Ezekiel 36:26).

The process of purification from sin requires true repentance and the restorative power of the Holy Spirit. God restores us spiritually by changing our hearts of stone into hearts of flesh, and we should also see modifications in our outward behavior, as well. Our new hearts and rebirth spiritually give us what we need to follow Him and execute His will in our lives and in the body of Christ.

As I come to the end of a year that at times seemed to move as if it were moving in slow motion and others moved at the speed of light, burning through my life like a supernova, I look back on all that my family and I have gone through, and it's easy to see that this has been a crushing season. A brutal journey from one trial to the other, and while it's easy to despair in the midst of it, I have to tell you: when you're in God's hands and He's the maestro, something amazing takes place. He fills you up with grace and equips you to fight through it.

I was talking to my daughter the other day, who came to me with tears in her eyes, really struggling with a difficult issue. I had none of the right words, couldn't stop the tears that flowed, and seemed to offer no words of comfort as she questioned whether God cared about her or loved her. I don't know if you have children, but even if you don't, you know the feeling of painful helplessness that comes when someone you love so deeply is in pain, and there's nothing you can do to stop it. But we are not common; we are not of the world and should not grieve or despair like the world. God's Word says that we ought to bear one another's burdens. So, as Christians, we have power unlike the world, the power given to us through Christ. We have a Savior who gave us the gift of salvation so that we can go boldly before the throne and intercede in prayer for those we love, care about, and encounter in our spiritual journey. Reaching out to brothers and sisters in Christ is a powerful weapon. We must remember God's Word in Matthew 18:19 says, "Again I say to you that if two of you agree on earth concerning anything that they ask, it will be done for them by My Father in Heaven." Jesus clearly instructs us here to join in prayer and that where two touch and agree, God moves, and power comes. See Matthew 7:7, Mark 10:35, and Luke 11:9.

There is power in unified prayer between two followers of Christ when we pray before God in Jesus's name. We don't have to have all the right words to say; we don't have to quote Scripture to the person who is hurting because, oftentimes, when people are in pain, they just need validation, comfort, a listening ear, or sometimes for you to say nothing at all. It took me reaching out to a dear friend who is like a sister to me and who I consider wise counsel to realize this, to know that I was not powerless to help my daughter but had one of the most powerful weapons given to man—prayers of intercession. It has the power to break yokes and set people free. It's easy to despair when trials come, but we don't have to let trials ruin us.

My daughter looked at me as if I were crazy when I said it had been a good year because she counted up all of the attacks and trials that we'd gone through in 2021, and they still seemed to be coming trying to disrupt and destroy our walk with God. But what I see as I look back on this year is God's faithfulness, the Red Seas He's parted, the walls that He's crumbled, the prison doors He's opened, and the warrior angels He's dispatched on my and my family's behalf. I see the growth that came from the testing; I see the great love He displays as He chastises and promises. God is faithful; He promised never to leave or forsake us. I've never felt His presence more up close and personal than while I've been going through it. He's also taught me that there's no shame in reaching out and asking for prayer because it's detrimental to suffer in silence. There's power in unity. Power in bombarding the throne. Jesus said, "Ask and keep on asking," in the parable of the persistent friend (Luke 11:9). Our Father knows what we need and how to provide for us, but just like a loving earthly father, He wants us to come to Him.

Psalm 50:15 says to call upon God in our day of trouble. We glorify God as He delivers us; that's what I'm experiencing. I exalt God and glorify His holy name because through every trial, painful as it has been, bawling through it, stumbling at times, being obstinate at times, God is a faithful Father, walking next to me, holding my hand, lifting me up and carrying me (when I was too distraught to carry on), picking me up when I've fallen and dusting me off. He's put up a shield all around me and hid me when I was too broken to fight and drew His sword when the enemy came around like a buzzard to finish me off. I've felt His love wrap around me like His very own arms held me, enveloping me in His amazing love. That's what I see when I look back on this year—not so much the trials but how God has brought me out and covered me. So, I look forward to the coming new year because I know what He's promised me and that He is faithful to deliver (Deuteronomy 7:9). And you should as well—the more you trust in God, the closer you walk with Him; He will bring things out of you that you never knew you had in you. He will strengthen you so that the next time the enemy tries to come for you, he'll flee seven before you. "The Lord shall cause thine enemies that rise up against thee to be smitten before thy face: they shall come out against thee one way, and flee before thee seven ways" (Deuteronomy 28:7), and you'll look back on trials and testing as moments of strengthening and growth.

Much of the work God does in us isn't to hurt us but rather to strengthen us and our dependence on Him. Think of a bodybuilder or strong man: he doesn't just wake up one day and say, "Today, I'm going to pull a semitruck with my bare hands"; no, he goes through strength training and preparation and builds the muscles to do it. So, God has to strengthen our spiritual muscles and build them up, and just as the process of building muscles works (by ripping, tearing, and repairing so that they can get bigger and stronger), our spiritual muscles are built—by trials and tribulation. But take heart, my friend, God will deliver you out of them all (Psalm 34:19). He may not always stop it, may not always bring you out of it, but rather through it for His purposes. Trust in Him: God never wastes anything; if He's allowing you to go through something, it's for a greater purpose than you know.

December 26, 2021

I was with my family for the holidays, and we went out for sushi on Friday night and placed our order from the restaurant's makeshift takeout window because they weren't letting people in if they were not dining in because of COVID-19. There was a woman who had been waiting for a while, and the man taking our order told us our order would be ready in twenty minutes. He then called the lady over to the window for her order pick up, and she stopped to tell us that the twenty-minute wait was a lie. She said that she'd called in her order, and they told her twenty minutes and that she'd waited over forty-five minutes for her food, then she wished us luck and left. I turned to my niece and my daughter, who were both waiting with me, and said, "Maybe for her, the wait was that long, but we're favored. The man said twenty minutes, and we will not be waiting longer than that!" As soon as I spoke it, the man at the pickup window called us over to retrieve our order. I was pleasantly surprised, not shocked, but why? God answered and showed me so that my niece could see, so we could all see that, indeed, those of us who are His are blessed and highly favored. That no matter how small we think a thing is, He inclines His ear to listen, hear, and answer us.

My daughter, niece, and I screamed when we walked away from the restaurant. God showed me in that very moment how close, how real He truly is. Whatever we ask, whatever we request of Him, if it is in His will, it will be done! So, I must be more mindful of God, and at times of stress, when we tend to go back to old habits or tools, we need to seek first the kingdom, to call out to God and seek His face; all else will be taken care of, even the little things we think don't matter (Matthew 6:33).

I was also reminded of some of the many promises God made to me, and that, too, settled me; knowing that you are safe in God's hands changes your outlook to the point where you no longer feel comfortable in the same old situations or moving in the same circles. When we put God first every day, no matter what is going on or what might be falling apart around us, we can trust that God will keep us in perfect peace as long as our minds are fixed on Him. I've noticed that when I don't make it a habit to pray when I wake up in the morning, read Scripture, and spend time in His presence, it is easy to get caught up in the pressures of the day. But when we spend time in worship, prayer, and before the throne, the enemy cannot reach us there.

January 8, 2022

What does "take up your cross and follow me" (Matthew 16:24–26) mean to you?

I was listening to worship music today, and the thought came to me. The Holy Spirit said to me that the burdens we take on and carry ourselves are too much for us because we were never meant to carry them, nor do we possess the power to fix them. These battles belong to God and are His domain (as He has told me many times); He is well able. In this scripture, Jesus means for us to lay down our earthly burdens at the foot of the cross and to take up what He has asked of us as part of the body of Christ because that is what He has given us the grace to do and fully equips us to handle. This means putting all of our trust in God in the midst of life's turbulent times and trusting that He will take care of the rest. What a comfort, right? That we don't have to worry because the God who breathed this world into existence and who knows our beginnings and our endings has us completely covered. That, my friend, is true peace.

February 7, 2022

Hidden Years

As human beings, we tend to grow impatient when we expect things to happen or move in our lives, and it all seems to be going at a snail's pace. Yet, we forget that God's timing is perfect, and nothing will happen before its time. Imagine if God gave us everything we wanted when we wanted it. Think about that for a minute. I can think about many things I wanted during my life and would have given anything to have them, yet in hindsight, I thank God that He didn't listen to me and saved me from myself. Sometimes we need to grow spiritually before God can give us much. Think about a caterpillar in a cocoon; it stays in that protected environment until all of the growth stages have been completed. It's not until the transformation process is completed that we see the new creature burst forth, beautiful and whole.

That's what God does for us when He hides us in a secret place while He's doing the work in us. He hides us from the outside until we are ready and His work at that stage is done in us, changing us into a new creation. A caterpillar (us with all of our bad behaviors and wrong thinking) ultimately turns into a beautiful butterfly.

Dot to Dot

God doesn't always give us the big picture. He takes us from one point to the other, one clue at a time, teaching us to trust Him each step of the way. As we connect each guidepost we pass, each season we go through and come out of, once all of the dots are connected, we can step back and see the beautiful picture created at the end.

I have learned so much this past week that I am amazed. I had been lamenting about still going to therapy because, at this point, I didn't feel like we were learning anything in marriage counseling that I hadn't learned in all my years of individual therapy. Yet last week, we had an interesting session where we didn't address any real issues except my husband bringing up how to discuss financial matters. I was so annoyed, and after the session, I asked my husband why he felt the need to blindside me instead of speaking with me directly. He said it's because he gets stressed out whenever he has to talk to me about finances because I get so angry. I was annoyed. We were able to discuss a few things, but I asked him to agree to discuss things no matter what; I could feel the Holy Spirit calming me because I was becoming agitated.

Then I realized that things that happened in the past (things my husband had done in our relationship to hurt me) caused me to develop behaviors and habits, putting up walls because of it. I realized I'd been holding onto these transgressions, which has caused me to be on the defensive when we discuss money. I know that God has been working on me in every area of my life! Exposing things in me and behaviors that I need to recognize and make a conscious effort to turn away from and allow the Holy Spirit to purge from me. Where God is taking us, I cannot keep thinking that I'm good and the work that needs to be done only needs to be done by my husband. I need to be humble enough to know that I must reflect inward and ask what God is trying to teach, show or change in me.

This week our refinance came through, and again we had some tense conversations because the bank mainly chose my debt to pay off. God asked me to think about how I would feel or behave if my husband was the one whose debts the bank decided to pay off instead of mine. Would I not want to bring up the unfairness? Of course, I would! I would harp on it and bring it up constantly until I felt things were equal or in my favor.

Then another thing happened this week; I found myself getting annoyed with my husband quite a bit and, at times, if I am being honest, being judgmental. Just because God is on my side in matters of infidelity, that does not give me carte blanche to act as if I'm perfect and without fault. God still has good work to do in me and is still revealing areas where I still need work. I thank God that I am at a place where I am now self-aware and humble enough to recognize the faults that are hindering my spiritual growth. The Holy Spirit also made me realize that I am unfairly expecting fruit from a sapling by treating my husband as if he is spiritually mature, forgetting that God still has work to do in him also. As Christians, we must be careful not to expect others to be where we are in our spiritual walk because each person's walk with God is individual and unique. I need to allow God to do His work and stop getting in the way; as my friend always tells me, I am not on the committee up in heaven, so I don't get a say. Yes, it has been a humbling week at every turn; God exposed old behaviors and habits that He wanted, no, needs me to quit.

February 16, 2022

Criticism, Judgment, and Slander

"Words": the Bible says in Proverbs 15:4, "Gentle words bring life and health; a deceitful tongue crushes the spirit." "Kind words are like honey—sweet to the soul and healthy for the body" (Proverbs 16:24). "Words satisfy the soul as food satisfies the stomach; the right words on a person's lips bring satisfaction" (Proverbs 18:20).

Our words have the power to build up and the power to tear down. We don't think about that when we are the ones speaking the words, but we ought to think about everything we say and ask ourselves how those words would make us feel. Do they build us up or tear us down in ways that go deeper than just hurt feelings? God tells us to mind our tongues because just as our words in prayer have the power to break yokes and fetters and set us free from bondage, they also can put us in bondage.

Yesterday was one of those difficult days for me as a mother. Though my children are all grown, there is still that deep desire within me to protect them from every evil thing in this world. Yet, I know that we serve a mighty God, there is none like Him, and He is the One who vindicates and fights for us. Did He not say we should hold our peace and let him fight our battles? I had to help my son resolve a problem with his auto insurance yesterday, and I called him to tell him that the issue was resolved, but I needed paperwork from him to complete the process. He sounded a bit tired when I called him, but that was common with him because he gets up every day at two a.m. to go to work. After I got done telling him what I had to say, I was prepared to say bye and hang up because he's not much of a talker when he is tired. He said to me, "Mom, so I had a really rough day today." He went on to tell me that he went to talk to a director about an engineering position that he'd been striving for. He's young, ambitious, and hardworking. He's been that way since he was a child, and anyone who truly knows him knows that. He told me that when he spoke to the director, the director told him that he had a "perception" problem. That he spoke with people who worked with my son who told him my son was unreliable, underachieving, and always waited to be told what to do. My heart broke into a million little pieces as he told me the things that were said. I knew it hurt him deeply because he cared about what others thought of him, and what they were saying was untrue.

We all do, if we are being honest; the goal is to care about what God thinks of us and what He says about us more than we do people. This is why God warns us to take care in what we say and to care about how we treat others: we've all heard the saying that we should treat each other with kindness because we don't know what battles a person may be fighting. I think about the headlines we've seen where a person was driven to do the unthinkable because of unkind, harsh, and hateful words that were spoken to them. We can speak just a word, and it could heal something broken in a person by just saying, "I care about you," or we can utterly destroy a person with just one hateful word. We need to care about the things that God cares about, and He cares about how we treat one another. Jesus said in Matthew 25:40, "And the King will answer and say to them, 'Assuredly, I say to you, inasmuch as you did it to one of the least of these My brethren, you did it to Me.'" I believe Jesus is telling us that how we treat others as His brothers and sisters shows our devotion to Him and our faith in Him. No matter how hard we try to seek validation and affirmations from others, only God can encourage and lift us up.

What I have realized is that this is God's way of drawing us closer to Him. We face problems that only He has the power to solve, and it draws us into communication with Him. God is always waiting for us to ask Him for help; His angels are always on standby, waiting on their orders to rescue us from the clutches of the enemy—we need only ask.

February 17, 2022

I was reading my daily devotional today, and the Holy Spirit honed in on what Christ endured on the cross. We often overlook what He dealt with: He went through a tumult of emotions: abandonment, shame, God's wrath poured out on Him, abuse, His friends turning their backs on Him; so, He fully understands our human condition, He knows all too well of the afflictions we face. The Bible is Jesus's roadmap showing us how to navigate these emotions and trials.

Yesterday was a tough day for my husband. He was being attacked unfairly by his boss and manager. Though I try to encourage him, I choose to take it to God in prayer. He is the only one who can vindicate us and defeat our enemies, but we must seek Him. God wants to give us His peace and comfort in knowing that we don't have to fight our battles on our own; He will! But we should not wait until all hell is breaking loose and we are crumbling under the weight of our problems to cry out to God. We should be in daily communication with Him through prayer and cast all of our burdens upon the One who sleeps, nor slumbers, and wields all of the power to defeat our enemies. God should not be someone who we have a casual re-lationship with, who we only pick up the phone to call when we want something from Him. He should be the first one we call on always! We must invite Him into our situations so that He can fix them; that's called a relationship. A relationship with God involves speaking to Him daily (prayer), depending on Him (trust), worship and praise (appreciation), and under-standing Him (through reading His Word, the Bible)—all of the same components that go into building relationships in the natural; the difference is He is all-powerful, all-knowing and knows us better than anyone. Think of your own relationships: you want someone to be with you because they love you, not because you forced them to be with you—that's not love. In the same way, God will not force Himself on us; imagine how pain-ful it is for Him to watch us stumble through life and situations on our own, knowing that He has the power to get us through or resolve the situation for us, but we never ask Him. As a par-ent, I find it heart-shattering.

It is our life experiences that qualify us to speak to others. No one wants to take advice from a person who hasn't gone through the troubles and testing they speak about. So, it is im-portant that we share our testimonies with others to strength-en, lift up, and give hope to others.

February 21, 2022

Yesterday was tough: hearing that I am a big part of the division in our family and the negative atmosphere among us. Hearing that I was wrong about how I treat my husband and that we make him feel that there is something wrong with him and exclude him when we have our private conversations. I feel so burdened like everywhere I turn, every stride that I make, I'm going in the wrong direction or doing the wrong thing. Each time I think I've grown or am doing what God is asking of me, I find out that I'm not. Sometimes I'm reluctant to say that I've heard from God or elaborate on anything because I get it wrong. I feel like just when I think I understand what God is asking of me, I find out that I have no clue. *Don't trust people*, but treat everyone with love and kindness, and don't get too comfortable. *Call out sin*, but don't judge. *Pray against your enemies* but pray for them. *Pray for people to be removed* but pray for their salvation and care about their souls. *Ask God for wisdom and let Him guide your steps* but don't wait for clarity or explanations; act on faith no matter what you see; even if you make a mistake, He will work it into His plan. If you believe you should have it, ask for it in prayer; you will receive it, but don't daydream.

God knows the turmoil I am feeling inside right now, so I am being honest: I have no idea what I'm supposed to be doing. I wonder if sometimes it's my own voice that I'm hearing and not God's. This is why Scripture tells us to be careful how we listen (Luke 8:18). When we misinterpret what we have heard, we can walk away with an incorrect understanding and make false assumptions. Instead of gaining more spiritual wisdom through asking questions, we lose what little spiritual light we have (spiritual confusion) because we fail to seek divine truth. This is when we should lean into God and seek the guidance of others who are more spiritually mature than we are.

February 23, 2022

The Sweet Aroma of Trials

God is oftentimes the author of our trials because there is always a purpose to them. He wants to press something out of us, something in our character, something about the way we think, perhaps the way we treat others, but something that He needs us to face and deal with and out of that time of trial, yields the beautiful aroma of change, a wonderful season of growth that refines us and strengthens us for the journey ahead. I remember watching my brothers play video games when we were younger. They would start out at a fairly easy level where the tasks are simple, and they get coins or weapons for the next stage. As they progressed, the stages got harder; they learned new skills and picked up important weapons for the tasks ahead. I watched them practice as they failed at the harder levels but kept going back and remembering the lessons they learned until they conquered the levels and advanced. This is how we ought to see our trials; at each stage, God is helping us to develop and strengthen ourselves, giving us weapons along the way to fight the next-level enemies we are about to face. If we fail the trial, there is nothing wrong with learning from our mistakes, picking ourselves up, dusting ourselves off, and trying again! It is important for our spiritual growth that we do not stay stuck at a level in our walk and do not want to go forward. That's how I felt yesterday—defeated and tired, battle-worn. But as a dear friend told me, we have to deal with our issues, or else they will later deal with us. There is no way around it but through it, and isn't it incredibly awesome that we have a Helper to go through it with us? In my brother's video games, the helper was tricks and tips they would learn from other friends or through the video game; we have a well-equipped, all-powerful Helper who came in the name of the One who has conquered all! We need to remember that while we go through the toughest of trials, though we may be battle worn, we are never defeated unless we give up!

We fall short when we work in our own power, but when we are obedient and depend fully on Christ, victory is inevitable. We need to ask for a fresh infilling of the Holy Spirit each and every day to be properly equipped for what lies ahead.

February 25, 2022

Unforgiveness

We live in a society that holds onto wrongs, dredges up the past of others, and judges them for it as if we don't change as we grow and mature. Even more importantly, when we are born again, our sins are wiped away, and we are made new, meaning God has forgiven and forgotten our sins and past transgressions, so how is it that we, who are but a vapor, put ourselves in the judgment seat of the almighty God and pass judgment on others? We must learn to forgive the transgressions of others just as we have been forgiven and saved by the work Christ did on the cross at Calvary. Why, then, do we listen to our flesh and are reluctant to give the same grace to others? I know it's hard, friend; God showed me today that I had forgiven my husband and not the people he cheated with. Withholding forgiveness is one of those things that can separate us from God, just like sin. What I mean is: it's a wedge between our loving Father and us that we must shed before we can fully come into His presence. It's like your child wanting to climb into bed to snuggle with you, but he or she is all covered in dirt and needs to take a bath first but doesn't understand why you're sending him or her off to the bath first. We are sons and daughters of the King, and He wants a relationship with us. We must work with Him on removing anything that gets in the way of that relationship.

March 27, 2022

There's nothing like a crisis to bring out what is hidden in the recesses of our minds and in the secret places of our hearts. Or a single storm to roll in that totally obliterates the progress you have made in your spiritual walk because you fail the test when trouble comes. Scripture says, "He who dwells in the shelter of the Most High, shall abide under the shelter of the Almighty" (Psalm 91:1). If we seek God always, especially when trouble comes, He will not allow anything to happen to His children and will send His angels to look after us (vs. 9–12). This past week was extremely challenging for my family and me. I know I say this quite a bit, but it seems like the enemy has sent a constant barrage against us since 2020. My husband ended up in the ER not once but twice with supraventricular tachycardia (faster than normal heart rhythm); the second time, he was admitted because he needed a cardiac ablation. He woke me up at 7:15 a.m. on a Monday morning and said, "We need to go to the ER now!" I jumped out of bed, brushed my teeth, got dressed, and drove as quickly as I could to the ER. We spent most of the morning there and went home in the early afternoon, only for him to feel faint and tight-chested again. So, back to the ER, we went at around 7 p.m. and never left because he was kept for observation. Both of us were tested because though I didn't want to be there and I was uncomfortable, he was irritable and rude because he didn't feel well, and of course, the enemy came slinking in at this opportune time. To give you a bit of back-story, my husband tends to act like a baby that I need to care for when he is not feeling well (not that I am minimizing what he went through because the triage nurse described the supra-ventricular tachycardia as his heart running a Nascar race and dragging his body along with it) and it has always irritated me in the past. With the stress of being in the emergency room, driving to the hospital every day to take care of him and sit with him, driving home at the end of the day, and trying to care for myself, I felt old feelings resurface, and the enemy started to sift through things that we believed were long gone but lay buried beneath the surface. God will often use these situations to show us that we have not truly addressed certain issues and have more work to do. The enemy told me that my husband didn't deserve my help, to look at what he did to me in the past, and I'm standing by him like a fool. But God's voice is louder than the enemy's, and I remembered what He said to me at the beginning of this current season when my husband admitted his infidelity—that I was keeping my promise to Him, not my husband. So, while it took a toll on me emotionally, physically, and mentally to drop everything and go to the hospital every day for eight hours or more each day, I'm grateful to God for not letting me stumble back into old spiteful habits because that is spiritual growth! My husband was not feeling well and was going through a potentially serious health crisis, and I, as his wife, treated him the way I would want to be treated and the way God would want me to, no matter what my flesh was saying to me. This was one of those situations where I firmly believe God's divine objective was at work.

These are the times when our faith is tested, and we need to dig deep into what we've learned through scripture and through Christ's example so that we can behave in a way that is "worthy of the Lord, fully pleasing to Him, bearing fruit in every good work and increasing in the knowledge of God" (Colossians 1:10, ESV). In this scripture, Paul is telling us that we should walk in a manner that reflects what God has done in our lives and is doing in us. So, others should see the difference walking with God made in our lives; they should not see the same person they once knew; remember: we are a new creation once we accept Christ, meaning we no longer behave the same way, talk the same, or move in the same environments as we once did.

April 1, 2022

I woke us this morning so worn out and drained because despite taking two Benadryl pills and going to bed early, my husband's snoring kept me tossing and turning and frustrated until almost 1 a.m. He then came to me, rubbing my shoulders as I sat at my desk, working, and telling me that I needed to take a day off, but in my mind, I was screaming and crying that what I needed was a day off from him! When testing and trials come, it is easy for us to give in to such feelings, easy for us to think "poor me" when instead, we need to press into God and the comfort that is at the throne waiting for us.

This latest round of testing has truly felt as if it was from the devil! But we know as Christian believers that this is not necessarily true. Sometimes God will test us to refine us, just as a goldsmith or silversmith puts gold or silver in the fire to refine it or to mold it into the desired shape, get out the impurities, and turn it into something precious and valuable. On its own, gold is a metal filled with impurities when it is first mined from the earth. Those impurities are removed through a common practice of placing scraps of gold into a crucible that is placed in a furnace burning at almost 1,366 kelvin, causing the gold to melt; then, the gold is poured into another container, and the impurities and other foreign materials float to the surface.

This is how God often uses trials in our lives to expose the impure thoughts, beliefs, and actions that hinder a deeper connection to God. His trials and fire strip us of our fleshly desires and break our flesh to draw us to Him. When we go through testing, our prayer lives improve and allow us to fully surrender to God's will. These past fourteen days have felt as if I was placed in the fiery furnace and left there, but like with the three Hebrew boys, Jesus was in the fire with me.

My husband woke up early two Mondays ago with a racing heartbeat that was so swift he nearly passed out. I had to rush him to the hospital, where they diagnosed him with supraventricular tachycardia, placed him on a beta-blocker, and gave him the option to go home or stay and have a cardiac ablation done; he chose the latter. Fast forward five hours after: taking the first dose of the beta-blocker caused his pressure to drop, and back we went to the ER. For the next five days, I was on a schedule of getting up early in the morning to head to the hospital to sit with him for eight hours or more, driving home in just enough time to eat dinner, shower, and go to bed to do it all over again. To him, I was just sitting there while he was the one going through it, but never did he consider what I had been going through, shouldering the stress of holding his hand, waiting on him hand and foot, and dealing with his sometimes rude and inconsiderate behavior because he was ill and afraid while doing it. I was running on empty by Wednesday, the day before he was scheduled for his procedure, and even more so when he said to me, "I want you to be here when I come back from surgery." I told him I would try. I was exhausted, so knowing that he would go in at 7 a.m. and his procedure would take three hours, I tried to get a few more hours of sleep. His doctor called me a little after 10 a.m. to say all went well and my husband would be in recovery for two hours and then would be back in his room.

With the extra time, I decided to take the time to do some of my own personal tasks that I had neglected to focus on during his health crisis. Then he called me around 11:45 a.m., very groggy, saying, "You were supposed to be here!" I explained to him that the doctor told me he was in the recovery area, so I took care of a few things that needed my attention. All he kept saying was that I was supposed to be there when he got out. I wanted to scream and tell him how selfish he was behaving, but I simply told him that I would be on my way. I went to take a shower, and everything came crashing down on me, and all I could do was cry.

It's times like these that test believers. How are you going to treat others when they don't treat you well? My flesh wanted to treat him the way he'd treated me and let him down the way he'd let me down, let him suffer for what he'd put me through, but would that be reflecting the image of God? Would others be able to see Christ in me? These are the kinds of behaviors that God wants to expose, the deeply buried habits that only rear their ugly heads when we are put in stressful situations; this is when our desire to please God needs to outweigh what pleases our treacherous hearts and our misguided feelings. We are called to be the light of the world so that others can be led to Christ, so we must remember it's not about us but about those whom we might encounter along life's journey who need to know that salvation awaits them. God breaks us in His consuming fire so that He can mold us into what He wants and needs us to be. This is how we die to our flesh, and if we persevere and grow in our faith by honoring God, He will reward and bless us. James reminds us in his book:

> My brethren, count it all joy when you fall into various trials, knowing that the testing of your faith produces patience. But let patience have its perfect work, that you may be perfect and complete, lacking nothing.
>
> James 1:2–4

God allows these testing and trials to prepare us for His plans and purposes for our lives. The meaning of the word refine in Hebrew is sublimate, delight, improve, make tender, sweeten. Another Hebrew word that I found interesting was *tsaraph*, literally meaning "to fuse" (Zechariah 13:9; Isaiah 48:10; Malachi 3:2–3). God wants to fuse us to Him by removing all impurities from our lives and bringing us back into the fold. *Tsaraph* also means "tried" (Psalm 66:10), "melt" (Jeremiah 6:29), and "purge" (Isaiah 1:25). When we go through testing and trials in life, God melts away the lies with His all-consuming fire, purges us of our wrong thinking and behaviors, and tries to ensure that we continue to grow and mature spiritually. We should count it all joy (James 1:2–3) (though it is painful) when we go through troubles because we know the result is God continuing to perfect us.

April 13, 2022

One of my favorite parts in the Bible is the one where Jesus meets John and his brother James and gives them the name Boanerges, "sons of thunder," in Mark 3:17, which I thought was such a cool name; however, when I realized the reason Jesus called them both sons of thunder was because they had details in their character that could be damaging to the people they were called to serve (they both had a fervid and impetuous temper [Luke 9:54]), my outlook changed. As their story progresses, we see a change in both brothers, a softer side that came about because they were under the influence and tutelage of Christ. God would not put us in places of influence over His flock without calling out and purging the habits or behaviors that could cause harm to those we are being chosen to help.

April 15, 2022

Good Friday

This year started off like a percussion instrument, and the band keeps playing. I feel as if I am being dragged from trial to trial instead of from glory to glory. It is such a frightening situation when you go through health issues, they don't stop (like one hit right after the other), and the medical doctors can't quite seem to put their finger on the issue. It can also be very difficult for the loved one who has to go through a crisis with the ill person because we're the ones getting up with them at 1 a.m. after falling asleep at 11 a.m. and driving to the ER. Imagine doing this for days on end, every week for five or more weeks. We don't realize the toll things can sometimes take on caregivers. We, too, suffer silently, which is why in some cases where a loved one is gravely ill and a spouse or significant other is caring for them, they can pass away before the one who is suffering from the illness. I just read a headline from the *Today* show that says that women are six times more likely than men to be separated or divorced soon after a serious diagnosis.

I find this so very heartbreaking because as I sit next to my husband's hospital bed in a chair with no padding that only has one position for hours on end, watching medical professionals come and go, and he's lying in bed, sleeping through it all while my eyes are as dry as sandpaper, yet whatever he needs, I do for him. Whether it's getting up to grab a blanket, getting a hospital gown for him to wear, or accompanying him to the bathroom because he is at risk of passing out—I do it all. Sometimes with a smile on my face and others, to be honest, through gritted teeth. We often forget that though we are Christians, we are still human, and all have sinned and fallen short of the glory of God (Romans 3:23), which is why we all need a Savior.

Does my husband deserve the love and care that I provide? Maybe and maybe not, but the bigger question is: Do any of us deserve the grace that Jesus's sacrifice has afforded us? None of us do, and yet still He died once and for all (1 Peter 3:18). God's Word teaches us to treat others with love and compassion and with a kind heart; because we do not have a right to judge or mistreat others.

Now I understand why at the beginning of this year, the Holy Spirit gave me three people in the Bible to study so far for the year: Esther, Joseph, Abraham, and Job. We should consider all that Job experienced, and yet, still he managed to say, "Though he slay me, yet will I trust him" (Job 13:15). How we handle these storms, the stance we take, and the posture we choose determine how we come out of it. We don't control the storms in life, but we can choose to trust in the One who does.

May 7, 2022

Wow! About last night: my husband was on his way home from a day of fishing with our youngest son, and on his way home, I called him to ask what we were going to have for dinner. As our conversation progressed, I asked him about details regarding plans we had to see his mother, who was visiting from up north, and it happened to fall on Mother's Day. He became agitated, and we began to get into a discussion that had the potential to become a full-blown argument. Prior to this discussion, I had mentioned to him that he should remember what his doctor told him about staying away from alcohol due to VT, or ventricular tachycardia, yet he drank anyway. To give you a little background:

> A heart rhythm is considered ventricular tachycardia if it has more than 100 beats per minute with at least three ventricular heartbeats in a row. It's caused by a malfunction in the heart's electrical system. Ventricular tachycardia may eventually lead to low blood pressure and ventricular fibrillation, a condition in

which the heart beats in a rapid, inadequate heart rhythm. In this condition, the heartbeat is so fast and irregular that it causes the heart to stop working. This can be fatal.[21]

He had a recent ablation done on his heart to correct the issue. When he drinks, his snoring is amplified, and me being a light sleeper, I either get woken up in fright because his snoring can often sound like a bear growling or can't sleep. I can usually get away with wearing headphones and listening to the sound of rain to drown out his snoring, but when he drinks, no matter how loud I turn up the rain in my headphones (which, by the way, is incredibly uncomfortable), I can still hear his snoring. So, I told him that the next time he drinks, he would need to sleep on the couch because it's unfair that I got no sleep the night before and was completely exhausted (and terribly cranky), and I know in hindsight that I, too, was not at my best and acting out of my flesh. The conversation spiraled and turned into what I knew were the beginnings of an argument and his accusing me of things that were not true. I could almost envision the enemy weaving lies into the words that I spoke previously and him receiving those lies as truth. I stepped back from the conversation and remained quiet; doing anything else would have brought out behaviors that I know are not pleasing to God. Something else was exposed in this situation. Sometimes, we think we have a handle on a thing, and all it takes is the right combination of all the wrong things to reveal that we still have areas that need work. Areas where we have not completely submitted to God.

I realized that I hadn't submitted to God when He let me know after talking to a friend of mine about how I prayed and asked Him to give me the $11,000 that I needed to invest in a project I believe He called me to do and not only did God answer my prayers but he gave the $11,000 to me three times over; but because I expected it to come a certain way, I missed it. It wasn't until I was updating my friend on what was happening in my life since we hadn't spoken in a while that she pointed out that I was being disobedient to God because He gave me what I prayed for, and I did not act on it. She reminded me that God wants to use me, but I'm making it so that He cannot because I'm not doing my part. It was then that the Holy Spirit brought back to my remembrance that the word He gave me for my husband was for me as well. He told me to tell my husband, "Obedience is better than sacrifice." For me, I get so afraid of making a mistake by moving or acting on something that I want and convincing myself that it's God that I don't move at all. This is a form of disobedience I've realized because when we allow the enemy to use fear against us, we allow him to steal the blessings that God has for us because we're not doing our part. I needed to submit my will to God and trust that His will be done, that He is big enough to catch me if I make a mistake or misstep, if I fall, and that He can use any mistake I make to help my spiritual growth and help others. I've realized that the fear I have stems from the wrong belief that I am not able to do the things that God is calling me to do and that I'm ill-equipped, forgetting that it is the Holy Spirit working through me that qualifies me to do exactly what God is calling me to do. Now I can see why God put the book of Matthew on my heart this week; in

Matthew 10:19, Jesus tells us that we should not worry about what we are going to say or how to say it when we are speaking about the gospel, because it is the Holy Spirit who will tell us what to say at the appointed time.

Matthew highlights some of the missteps the disciples made, how they sometimes got it wrong, and how Jesus counseled, corrected, and encouraged them. They, too, sometimes had doubts and showed fear. When we are called and sent out in the name of Jesus Christ as His representatives, we will face all manner of trials, but going through these trials gives us a testimony to share with others and an opportunity to share the gospel with nonbelievers.

January 19, 2022

Scripture says that God knows the end from the beginning. The end of this book was given to me on January 19, well before I was done writing it.

It's amazing how, when we give God a try, meaning—coming to the end of ourselves and stop striving against God, understanding that we can do nothing in our own strength, and giving our mess over to Him—He is able to take that shattered thing that we have been trying to put back together on our own and restore it—not back to its original state as we knew it—but in the state that He meant for it to be. God will take that thing and make it shiny and new to where you cannot even tell that it was damaged at all.

When my father, who was my entire world, passed away in 2016 from ALS, I felt as if I was irrevocably broken. I cried in the shower with tears that came from a new place deep inside of me. I prayed from a place of desperation for God to do the miraculous and heal him. I did not know what I would do without him: Daddy was everything to me. He was larger than life, my confidant, my cheerleader, my wise counsel, my protector; he would do anything for me if I asked, all while pouring so much love into me that I know what true love looks like. I watched this titan of a man be ravaged by this cruel disease to the point where I could not recognize the man I saw before me but for that sparkle in his beautiful brown eyes that mirrored my own. That sparkle remained even after his speech had left him. I cried for the man he used to be because I could only imagine how incredibly difficult this experience was for him, a man who was so full of life, who did not look his age, a man who was so active, who commanded board rooms, a man who was a great communicator, a man who built corporations. I was amazed by his attitude throughout the whole thing; despite the bouts of tears and moments of sadness, my daddy looked at me and said, "Do you know what I am grateful for?" I was able to read his lips and listen to the sounds he made as he tried to speak to me; God is truly amazing because I understood every word he said and asked him what it was that he was grateful for. He said, "Despite all of this, the one thing God has preserved is my mind." I was blown away. My father, who was in the greatest battle of his life, found a blessing in his situation. I did not see it through my pain at the time, but God's sovereign hand was in it all.

I found out about my father's diagnosis in March 2016, and he passed away in August 2016. I went to his house in Orlando almost every other weekend to spend time with him, and today, I thank God for those moments. I look back and see the grace with which my father handled his diagnosis and remained hopeful and now realize that God's grace was with him.

I now see my father's battle as a lesson about how to handle the many things we face in life: submit ourselves to God's will, humble ourselves, obediently seek God through prayer and through His Word, and let Him fight our battles. Trust that He will only give us His best and believe that no matter what it looks like, He will bless and keep us.

I got quite ill after my father's funeral and was sick for an entire month after that because I felt as if a piece of me had died with him. I had gone through what I thought was heartbreak early on in my life, but I didn't know what a truly broken heart felt like until my father passed away. My heart was destroyed, and I felt like a rudderless ship; I was lost. My spirit was crushed because I felt like God didn't hear my prayers and didn't answer them. But God reached into my pain and despair and changed the way I saw things. I began to see how God's calling my father home was truly a gift because there was no more pain, no more ALS, no more depending on others to do the simplest of things that he could no longer do for himself; he was with the Father! Daddy would not have wanted to live his life bound to a wheelchair, unable to speak or move on his own, in constant pain feeling like a prisoner in his own body, so I am thankful and feel incredibly blessed to have had him in my life for as long as I did.

Jesus tells us in John 11:25–26 (NIV), "I am the resurrection and the life. The one who believes in me will live, even though they die; and whoever lives by believing in me will never die." In this scripture, Jesus tells us that He is the resurrection for those who have died because He will raise them from the dead and that He is the life for those who believe and are still alive when

He returns. So, though we mourn our loved ones, we rejoice in the knowledge that they will live again!

Paul reminds us in Philippians 4:8–9 (NIV),

> Finally, brothers and sisters, whatever is true, whatever is noble, whatever is right, whatever is pure, whatever is lovely, whatever is admirable——if anything is excellent or praiseworthy——think about such things. Whatever you have learned or received or heard from me, or seen in me——put it into practice. And the God of peace will be with you.

We must remember that what we feed ourselves (spiritually) determines the fruit of our words, actions, what we desire, and ultimately how we believe. We ought to be mindful of what we take in (on TV, what we read, what we listen to, etc.) and instead focus on pure and good things. We need to do more than just read the Word of God; we need to put what we learn into practice. It is easy for us to hear a good word on Sundays and, when we leave the church, to forget the seed that was planted. Hearing the Word and studying it should make us reflect on how we can live differently if we live according to God's Word. Therefore, we should not believe, speak, behave, or mourn the way the world does.

It took years for me to see my father's battle with ALS and untimely death differently. Each year, the pain of him not being here was unbearable. It took me studying the Word of God to see things through the lens of Scripture and take heart in knowing that my father though he died, will live again; knowing this gave me great comfort and peace.

That is why it is so important for us to know God and have a personal relationship with Him through Jesus. We cannot expect to know anything about God through others; we have to get to know Him for ourselves by seeking Him (spending time with Him) and reading His Word to know His character and what He has promised us.

The truth is that it was not until after I was saved that I realized that God gave us an example of what true love is. In John 3:16, He shows us what it really means to love. Jesus did not come to save only those who believed that He is the Messiah or to save God's chosen; He came to give *all* a path back to the One who first loved us. Jesus died once and for *all*. God sacrificed His one and only Son so that anyone (whosoever) who believes in Him has a chance at everlasting life.

January 20, 2022

My dear friend, in the end, we must remember that we cannot do life without God. I will share one last story with you. A few years ago, while I was still traveling an hour and twenty minutes one way to go to work, I would pack everything that I thought I needed for work (planners, bills, my fancy pens, books to read, the kitchen sink—you name it) and it filled a large purse, a large tote and my lunch would go into a lunch box that could probably have fed a multitude. My husband and children would look at me as if I were a crazy person loaded down like a pack mule. I also loved wearing three-to-five-inch heels because I'm 5'7" and my husband is 5'11", so you could imagine work was one of those rare occasions that I would get to wear my heels. At my office building, there was a short but steep flight of stairs with a handrail that went down from the garage to the third-floor door that led into the building. Because I did not want to make two trips to my car, I would load a bag on each shoulder and hold my lunch tote in one hand. I started down the small flight of stairs, and just as I got to the landing near the door to the building, I stepped awkwardly, and my foot wobbled, and I went down like a ton of bricks. Thankfully, I fell on my hands and knees. I was horrified to hear a voice say, "Are you okay?" And when I looked up, there was a young man who came through the door the instant that I fell. I was so embarrassed that I did not accept the young man's help. I told him that I was fine and pushed myself up to my feet, grabbed my things from the floor, thanked him, and pushed through the doors into the building, praying that no one was behind me and saw my graceless fall.

It was not until many years later that I was telling my dear friend about the incident during one of our Bible studies that later on that night, during prayer, God told me that it was me doing life without Him. That was such an amazing, eye-opening moment for me! That was me stumbling and falling through life without walking in lockstep, arm in arm with Jesus. My friend, I do not want you to wait until there is a crisis that brings you to your knees to seek God. I want you to seek Him with all your heart and build a meaningful relationship with Him. He does not want to see His children stumbling around this life like lost sheep surrounded by vicious wolves. He is the One who carries us when we can't go any further, who leads us down a righteous path, and if we do fall, He's the One that picks us up, brushes us off, and says, "Let's try again, My child."

Having God so near to me and letting Jesus lead me has been the anchor that kept what I have gone through these past two years from breaking me and doing more damage. We have an enemy who wants to set and bind us in chains, but we serve a chain-breaking, yoke-destroying Savior! But first, we must accept Him and serve Him to obtain those benefits. Let today be the day that you make the decision to accept Jesus Christ as your Lord and Savior and, if you are already saved and may have strayed from the path, to renew your relationship with Him. Jesus said, "I am the Way, the Truth, and the Life. No one can come to the Father except through Me."

He is our gateway, y'all, our path to the throne of grace to receive everything that He promises in the Bible. Won't you seek Him today? Freedom awaits you, my friend.

Be encouraged, be blessed, and most of all, I pray that this book has helped set you free. God wastes nothing; everything we experience in life has a divine purpose, and we discover this when we partner with and are rooted in Christ.

Notes

1   *Strong's Concordance*, s.v. "1588. eklektos," Bible Hub:
    Search, Read, Study the Bible in Many Languages, accessed
    May 20, 2022, www.biblehub.com/greek/1588.htm.
2   "What Is the Biblical Meaning of the Word 'restoration'?"
    Ask Media Group, LLC, last updated March 25, 2020, www.
    reference.com/world-view/biblical-meaning-word-restora-
    tion-436ed0eb2e3b3d0c.
3   Dictionary.com, LLC, s.v. "criticism," accessed May, 23,
    2022, www.dictionary.com/browse/criticism.
4   *Strong's Concordance*, s.v. "3528. nikaó," Bible Hub: Search,
    Read, Study the Bible in Many Languages, accessed May 23,
    2022, www.biblehub.com/greek/3528.htm.
5   Dictionary.com, LLC, s.v. "insecure," Dictionary.com, LLC,
    accessed May, 23, 2022, www.dictionary.com/browse/ inse-
    cure.
6   James Strong, *Strong's Exhaustive Concordance of the Bible*
    (Peabody, Massachusetts Hendrickson Publishers Market-
    ing: 2007).
7   *Merriam-Webster.com Dictionary*, s.v. "bear," accessed Octo-
    ber 6, 2022, https://www.merriam-webster.com/dictionary/
    bear.
8   "Do Your Best to Glorify Jesus | A Blessed Morning Prayer
    to Begin Your Day," Grace for Purpose Prayers, You-
    Tube video, October 14, 2021, https://www.youtube.com/

watch?v=l7ECmn7LOo4.

9 *Nelson's Compact Series Bible Commentary* (Nashville, Tennessee: Thomas Nelson, Inc., 2004) p. 434.

10 Dictionary.com, LLC, s.v. "intimacy," Lexico.com, accessed May, 23, 2022, www.lexico.com/en/definition/intimacy.

11 "KJV Dictionary Definition: scaffold," accessed October, 6, 2022, https://av1611.com/kjbp/kjv-dictionary/scaffold.html.

12 *Strong's Concordance*, s.v. "6862. tsar," Bible Hub: Search, Read, Study the Bible in Many Languages, accessed May 23, 2022, www.biblehub.com/hebrew/6862.htm.

13 *Merriam-Webster.com Dictionary*, s.v. "grace," accessed May 23, 2022, www.merriam-webster.com/dictionary/grace.

14 Dictionary.com, LLC, s.v. "Synonyms of *doubt* in English," Lexico.com, accessed May, 23, 2022, www.lexico.com/synonyms/doubt.

15 James Strong, *The Strongest Strong's Exhaustive Concordance of the Bible*, s.v. "fearfully," "wonderfully" (Grand Rapids, Michigan: Zondervan, 2001).

16 *Oxford Dictionary of Current English*, Fourth Edition (Oxford University Press: 2006).

17 "The Importance of Marking Anniversaries," Awareness Centre Limited, accessed May, 23, 2022, www.theawareness-centre.com/anniversaries.

18 *Strong's Concordance*, s.v. "3811. *paideuó*," Bible Hub: Search, Read, Study the Bible in Many Languages, accessed May 23, 2022, www.biblehub.com/greek/3811.htm.

19 James Strong, *Strong's Exhaustive Concordance of the Bible* (Peabody, Massachusetts: Hendrickson Publishers Marketing, 2007).

20 Dictionary.com, LLC, s.v. "submit," accessed October, 6, 2022, www.lexico.com/en/definition/submit.

21 "What is ventricular tachycardia?" Healthline.com, last updated on February 15, 2022, www.healthline.com/health/ventricular-tachycardia.

About the Author

Donya Gonzalez is a writer and author of the children's book *How Real Is God?* She was born in the Bahamas and currently lives in Florida. Donya has an MFA in creative writing from National University, and *Divine Purpose* is her second book, available wherever books are sold.